160

D0551482

WITHDRAWN

The Nature of Criticism

The Nature of Criticism

COLIN RADFORD
Reader in Philosophy,
University of Kent at Canterbury

and

SALLY MINOGUE
Lecturer in English,
Thanet Technical College

THE HARVESTER PRESS · SUSSEX
HUMANITIES PRESS · NEW JERSEY

First published in Great Britain in 1981 by
THE HARVESTER PRESS LIMITED
Publisher: John Spiers
16 Ship Street, Brighton, Sussex
and in the USA by
HUMANITIES PRESS INC
Atlantic Highlands, New Jersey 07716

© Colin Radford and Sally Minogue, 1981

British Library Cataloguing in Publication Data

Radford, Colin
  The nature of criticism.
  1. Art criticism
  I. Title   II. Minogue, Sally
  700′.1   NX640

  ISBN   0–7108–0082–7

  Humanities Press Inc
  ISBN 0–391–02273–3

RADFORD

UWIST
CARDIFF
library
21 MAY 1981
ACCESSION NUMBER 146285
CLASS NUMBER 801.95

Typeset by Inforum Ltd, Portsmouth
Printed in Great Britain by
St Edmundsbury Press, Bury St Edmunds, Suffolk

All rights reserved

To Judy

Contents

Introduction

The relationship between scholarship and criticism. Why criticism is intellectually exercising; why critics should be exercised by it. We shall be particularly concerned with critical disagreements.   1

The structure and methodology of this book. Central concern with criticism of literature.   6

Chapter One   The complexities of critical judgements.   8

1 A banal classificatory judgement may conceal moral and evaluative dimensions.   8

2 Can the usual distinction between what is banal and what is true be preserved in criticism? Response terms. Can works of art establish moral truths?   10

3 Certain assumptions underlie even a banal interpretative judgement about the literal sense of a work.   17

4 The basis of an incontestable interpretative claim about the non-literal significance of a work. Allegory as an example. The role of information external to the text.   18

5 The basis of a contestable interpretative claim about a work's non-literal significance. Different role of external information in different cases. Historicity of art objects.   21

6 Difficulties where an irrefutable judgement about the literal sense of a work coincides verbally with a problematic judgement about its deeper significance.   24

7 How do we decide between different interpretative claims both of which have a basis in the literal sense of the text? (This question is considered further in the following three sections.) The role of critical principles.   25

8 Where two interpretative judgements are supported equally by the literal sense of the work, it may be that neither is wrong. 'Seeing an aspect'. Differing roles of knowledge about author's intention in such cases.   27

9 Consistency with the literal sense of a work is not a sufficient condition for an interpretative judgement's being tenable. Role of connotations of words in a work. (Example: critical views of Andrew Marvell's 'To His Coy Mistress'.)   30

10 Why some interpretative judgements are inconsistent with literal sense. Is consistency with literal sense a necessary condition for a judgement's being tenable? The attraction of complexity for modern critics. (Example: critical views of Gerard Manley Hopkins' 'The Windhover'.)   33

11 Critics may agree in their interpretation of a work but disagree in their evaluation of it; such a disagreement cannot be resolved by appeal to the text. Critical disagreement may conceal a moral conflict; role of moral considerations in criticism. The cogency of these critical arguments depends on how we respond when we read the work. (Example: critical views of D.H. Lawrence.)   39

Chapter Two   The nature of critical arguments.   44

1 What is the nature of a critical argument? (Example: the arguments of F.R. Leavis and R.H. Fogle in their disagreement over Shelley.) Nature and location of the disagreement. Relationship between feature and effect in Leavis' argument more than causal. Fogle's method of reply. In Leavis' 'argument' the conclusion is logically prior to the particular observations made in support of it. Ways of replying other than Fogle's still encounter this difficulty.   44

Is Leavis' then an argument at all? Priority of 'conclusion' is not peculiar to critical argument. Distinction between critical and scientific arguments. Agreement between critical responses is the basis of the objective idiom of critical discourse.   48

Logical relationship between Leavis' critical terms and his evaluative judgements. Is the connection between trait and evaluation immediate, or do the two 'go together'? His terms are context-bound. Consequent difficulties of articulating a disagreement with Leavis. Some critical terms are general in their meaning but can be fully understood only through their use in particular cases; Leavis' terms may be of this sort. These terms are not used as criteria. Leavis' insistence that appeal to criteria is inappropriate in criticism.   50

Seeing an aspect; but we can't see anything as anything. We do sometimes argue *to* an aesthetic appreciation. The Leavis/Fogle disagreement is not necessarily characteristic.   54

2 Certain interpretative judgements, including some which have been chronically debated, can be shown to be correct. Features of the work which explain the continuing disagreement. The presence of a feature in a work is not sufficient for its having the effect suggested by the critic. (Example: critical views of Milton's style.)   56

3 Is it appropriate to put an experimental construction on

critical explanations? The correctness of an ostensibly
substantial claim depends on its being accepted. Yet acceptance
may then generate the substance. This meta-critical thesis is an
empirical one. (Example: Cleanth Brooks on Housman.) 62

4 How do we decide whether a critical explanation is correct
(assuming the truth of what is to be explained)? The attraction
of an explanation. A plausible explanation may 'create' the
response it seeks to explain. (Example: Christopher Ricks on
Milton.) 65

5 Detailed examination of the possibility of experimentally
testing a critical explanation. (Example: a claim by J.
Stallworthy about W.B. Yeats' 'A Coat'.) 68

Chapter Three *The logical richness of criticism; an
analysis of Ricks on Tennyson.* 84

A comprehensive analysis of a sustained piece of criticism and
fuller discussion of some large problems already raised.
(Example: Ricks' criticism of part of Tennyson's *In
Memoriam*.) 84

Complexity and ambiguity of apparently straightforward
claims. Compression and interfusion of different dimensions of
critical remarks. 89

Critical terms may not be univocal, even within a single piece of
criticism; 'interpretation' as an illustration. 90

Logical relationships between and within claims. A detailed
examination of the relationship between a feature and the effect
Ricks claims it has (his claim about the effect of an abba rhyme
scheme). 92

The normative dimension of critical argument; does not rule
out but rather presupposes and requires a causal dimension.
The role of common sensibility and general connections.
Distinction between natural and conventional connections. The
difficulty of isolating the effect of individual features in works
of art. When does hyper-acuity become over-sensitivity? 101

A claim where the presence of a feature is problematic (Ricks'
claim about the 'subterranean idea'); factors which decide
whether or not we accept the claim. 105

Comparison of the relationship between the 'subterranean idea'
and our response with the relationship between the rhyme
scheme and our response. Cause and target. Moral dimension
of our response to the 'subterranean idea'. 107

Danger of inflation of a feature in critics' description of it;
general danger of over-reading and 'creative' criticism. 113

Chapter Four   *Are there any necessary conditions of
excellence in art?*   115

Are there any necessary conditions of excellence in a particular
genus, drama? Unities of time and place, credibility, and unity
of action, considered (and rejected). Reasons for difficulty of
finding such necessary conditions.   115

Are there any 'local' necessary conditions of excellence within a
particular species of genus? Funniness in comedy considered;
not a formal notion, so it leaves room for disagreement, and is
too close to being tautological to be useful as a criterion.   123

Connection between a work's being a good one of its species, a
good one of its genus, and a good work of art.   123

Are there any necessary conditions of excellence in works of
art? Skill and originality considered. Reply to the objection that
they are irrelevant because they are 'genetic' qualities. Too close
to being tautological to be useful as criteria.   125

Are there any more substantial criteria? Clive Bell's 'significant
form' considered (and rejected).   129

Monroe Beardsley's definition of objective reasons; objections
to his exclusion of genetic, moral and cognitive qualities. His
canons of complexity, unity and intensity, are supported by his
definition of aesthetic experience. This definition is both too
exclusive and not sufficiently particular. Problems of
subsuming particular qualities of works under the canons;
disagreement always possible. The danger of 'freewheeling
rationalisations'.   131

Conclusion that it is unlikely that there are any criteria of
excellence in works of art. Thesis that aesthetic objects and
judgements lack an essence.   138

Chapter Five   *Reasons, causes and targets.*   141

A detailed critique of two opposed monolithic views of criticism
(Beardsley's that critical reasons must be general; Isenberg's
that critical remarks are logically singular.)   141

The work is characteristically both the cause and the target of
our response.   147

Acknowledgements   159
Notes to the Text   161
Index   177

Introduction

What sort of activity is criticism? A great deal of what the critic does is theoretically uninteresting, because it is unproblematic, for he is often in his capacity as a critic simply concerned with giving factual information about works of art, and with correcting misinformation about them. We will expect the Milton critic, for example, to know his Milton; he will be familiar with the texts and have an understanding of them which, among other things, will enable him to make syntactical difficulties and verbal archaisms intelligible to his reader. Of course, 'understanding' the text, and passing on that understanding, cannot be seen simply as a matter of scholarly expertise or factual knowledge; at times these qualities are tied up almost indistinguishably with a deeper, more personal understanding of what an author is saying, and the element of interpretation which this introduces raises theoretical problems. It would likewise be mistaken to think that even scholarship is always 'objective'; for scholars can have their idiosyncracies of approach which may influence how they see the work. But whilst we are aware of the problems which such factors can raise even in the most fundamental criticism, nevertheless it is on the whole theoretically unexercising; and not only unexercising, but often of little interest to the professional critic, except the scholar and the pedagogue. The professional critic is interested in the kind of criticism which at points merges with but which more usually *presupposes* their knowledge and understanding. Nonetheless, criticism of the more basic sort is important, because it is a prerequisite for 'higher criticism', and almost all professional critics spend a great deal of time engaged in it.

These two facts may help to explain why critics are characteristically not exercised by the nature of their own activity. The unproblematic nature of what is fundamental may conceal the methodological problems of the more subtle, and

1

more exciting, tasks which the critic sets himself.

Both the simple and the more complex tasks — both basic and higher-order criticism — consist in mediating between works of art and their audience; in making it possible for the reader to respond to the work, or where he can already respond perhaps without fully understanding the work, making the work more intelligible; in accounting for the reader's response in terms of the work itself; and even in creating that response, the response that the work, as he sees it, demands. The more subtle, difficult, and exciting part of his task consist largely in getting his account right, or, where the question of its being 'right', or 'wrong' seems irrelevant, in understanding why this should be so.

Thus criticism has the possibility of being a most important activity, for two reasons. In the first place, works of the imagination, though we might not be pleased to call all of these works of art, figure largely in the lives of almost all men. It's not every person that reads novels, but most of those who do not, do watch television or go to the cinema. Given this pervasive interest in works of the imagination it will follow that criticism might have an important social role to play.

This social claim about criticism may not be warranted; it may well be that most academic critics anyway write, for the most part, for each other and that they don't create taste but follow it;[1] but we shall not argue about this. It is the other fact which makes criticism intellectually exercising, *viz*. the kind of claim it makes about works of art.

The critic wants to give an account of works of art which goes beyond the brute level of saying what is there. A critic looking at Gainsborough's portrait of Sarah Siddons might say, 'Isn't she sad'; and if we look at the portrait again in the light of this remark we might agree, and wonder why we did not notice the sadness before. Though the critic's remark is of a very different order than his telling us, say, that the woman in the painting is wearing a black hat, nevertheless the quality of sadness is as much there for him as is the hat, and we may accept the powerful truth of his claim as readily as we would accept the more factual statement. Certainly we derive much more interest and help from it. But how can such a quality be claimed so certainly to be 'in' the painting (even if we were to settle the question of whether the critic is attributing the sadness to Mrs. Siddons herself, the person behind the portrait, or to the painted face for which Mrs. Siddons happened to be the model)? For the face is in repose and, in that sense, is expressionless.

Not only does the critic want to make interpretative claims about works of art; he also wishes to tell us how we respond to these works. It may seem puzzling that a man might tell us how we respond to something, and sometimes it may be that he assumes our response to be the same as his — 'Don't we feel like this?' His account, then, couched though it is in terms of 'how we respond', carries an implied 'should'. So that sometimes the critic is telling us how we should respond to works, which in turn raises problems about the force of the often suppressed but implied 'should'. What kind of 'should' is it, and what is its provenance? Is he telling us that this is the morally proper response; or is he telling us merely that this is how an accurate reader would respond; or a reader of fine intelligence and sensibility; or is it some combination of these?[2] Except, perhaps, where the 'should' is a moral one, saying 'This is how you should respond' is like saying 'This is what is there'. We return to the problem mentioned above. And this task, of saying how we do or should respond, is not easily separated from yet another, where a critic will try to give some account of why works of art affect us — why we respond to a particular work as we do, what it is in the work which arouses our responses.

So criticism is a problematic activity, and further intellectual problems are raised by the particular nature of the claims sometimes made by critics working in our tradition. They make claims and counter-claims with equal vehemence and equal certainty in critical disputes, and are apparently unaware of any incongruity in this. And even the claims which are undisputed, which are generally agreed on, can be puzzling. Rembrandt's 'honesty', his avoiding sentimentality in his portraits, is generally accepted and acclaimed by those familar with his work, and it is this, rather than mere technical facility, which explains his stature. But how can we say this when we do not know anything about, for example, the character or appearance of Jan Six? Yet wouldn't such knowledge be irrelevant to the truth of the claim? What then can be its status?[3] Or again, a critic might explain part of the appeal of Matthew Arnold's 'Dover Beach' by saying that the irregular rhythm of the lines echoed the irregular rhythm of the waves. But while it is true that the waves may sometimes beat in the same irregular rhythm as the lines of the poem, this is clearly insufficient to establish that this explanation of the appeal of the poem is correct. But what *would* be sufficient, or, indeed, relevant?

It should strike us as curious, though it usually does not, that we characteristically do not seek evidence or proof of such claims when reading criticism; we merely agree, or disagree. May it be that our accepting the explanation is itself sufficient for its being correct, if we can speak of correctness here? But how can this be so? If we do not proceed in such a manner when doing criticism, doesn't this suggest that this activity characteristically lacks rigour?

Besides offering explanations for which they give no support, critics also say that works of art are not simply aesthetically pleasing, or otherwise; novels, plays, poems, paintings — especially portraits — even music, are also claimed to contain, and to reveal to any sympathetic audience, profound truths about the human condition.[4] Again, the reader of criticism does not usually baulk at such claims or seek to test their correctness. Indeed, sympathy with views of this kind is not confined to, or even produced by, professional criticism. We get the impression that persons who do not read criticism are prepared to go even further than the professional in this area. They will often feel that these truths are not simply truths about life, but truths which do not require corroboration from life. The works seems to reveal them immediately. But how can this be?

Yet the fascination that works of the imagination hold for us is not simply to be explained in terms of an acceptance of the belief that some of these reveal profound truths about what it is to be human. Works of art are aesthetic objects, that is to say, they are created with the intention that they should give pleasure in their manner of expression whether or not they contain profound truths. And the intense and lasting nature of our response to this aesthetic dimension is exercising — just because it is so complex, and difficult to give an account of. Sometimes this response may even seem disproportionate — what is the nature of the appeal of a brief Mediaeval lyric, such as 'I sing of a maiden', for it to have survived several hundred years, and still be arousing an intense emotional and aesthetic response? Criticism is concerned with trying to give some account of the nature of a response such as this, with making it more intelligible to us, and thereby dissipating, not our central interest in works of art, but the puzzling nature of that interest.[5]

Criticism, then, attempts much and demands much. It is commonly, and primarily, regarded as requiring not merely scholarship, but fine intelligence and as part of this an acute moral sensibility. It is therefore a difficult task which makes large demands on its practitioners. But, if we are right, it is also difficult to do well if the very nature of what is essayed by critics is often questionable.

These facts suggest that critics would do well to be aware of what they are doing. But as we mentioned earlier, there is reason for thinking that, however sensitive as critics, they are not particularly interested in or exercised about the activity itself. They may even be hostile to a critical interest in criticism — cf. F.R. Leavis' response to R. Wellek.[6] In this respect they resemble most psychoanalysts, apparently taking the line that no-one can have true understanding of the activity unless he practises it, and that practice is sufficient for understanding and validation. But although we may accept the first claim, we cannot accept the second.

As a result of this attitude, the way in which critics approach their own activity often suggests that they misunderstand it. This is not surprising, or even reprehensible. Critics are, understandably, obsessively concerned with the work itself, and they have no professional training in, for example, the now highly developed philosophy of explanation. Still, the lack is there, though it would not matter if there were no reason for feeling doubtful about the activity.

Our interest, then, in criticism, and so our discussion, is mainly with what is problematic. This explains our particular interest in critical disagreements, for the curious nature of the critic's claims, and of what he can appeal to when those claims are challenged, is most clearly revealed when critics disagree. But these problems are not restricted to such cases — mere agreement does not dispel them. And our first examples are of judgements far removed from critical dispute — they are of judgements which are so generally accepted as to be banal, so banal that professional critics would probably not bother even to state them, but would assume them in their discussion of the works in question. The points we make about such judgements may strike the practical critic as unreal; but it is important to analyse what underlies such judgements, just because the less disputed the judgement, the deeper we must go to discover its basis, and the less considered that basis by the person who makes the judgement.

A final word about our method: works on aesthetics are usually highly theoretical, abstracting various critical concepts from the business of criticism itself. They use terms for these concepts — 'interpretation', 'evaluation', 'description', etc. — as though the terms had meanings identifiable separately from particular critical judgements. But, as we shall show, what is meant by 'description', 'interpretation', 'evaluation', etc. tends to vary from one bit of criticism and one critical controversy to another. We may be clear about what we mean by 'interpretation' in one case, but unclear as to whether we would mean the same thing by that word in another case. At the same time, a critical remark is often at once a description of a work, an account of how the critic feels and why, a justification and explanation of his view, and hence what he would say in arguing with a critic who held a rival view; and these various dimensions may be difficult to separate, yet the logical relationships between them may be elusive and complex, and particular to the case in question. Thus an account of criticism in terms of 'interpretation', 'evaluation', etc. would be academic. We must proceed by examining particular cases of critical judgement to understand these various dimensions and the relationship between them. This way of proceeding also reveals that criticism is not a monolithic activity, but a motley of cases.

In our first two chapters, then, we simply examine a variety of critical judgements and arguments and the problems arising from them. This necessary procedure has one disadvantage: we see criticism piecemeal whereas when we read a piece of criticism it is usually sustained, and its effect may depend partly on that. In Chapter Three therefore, we look at an extended passage of criticism, and take that opportunity to give a more comprehensive account of some of the problems raised in the previous chapters. If general claims about the nature of criticism are implicit in these discussions, their correctness, the extent to which they apply, can only be established by looking at further examples.

Of course, many of the questions do raise large-scale 'theoretical' problems which the examination of particular bits of criticism can scarcely solve; while we tackle these problems as they arise from particular examples, and thus build up an account 'from the field', we move to a more theoretical examination of them in our last two chapters.

A final point: our emphasis is on the criticism of literature, for that is where we have knowledge and what most academic criticism is concerned with.

1 The complexities of critical judgements

We shall begin by examining examples of judgements which, as criticism, are banal, and show that, despite this fact, and their superficial grammatical appearance which is descriptive or classificatory, making them raises various large issues, which we discuss. Next we examine some of the problems raised by judgements which, as criticism, are more interesting and complex. In the latter half of this chapter we shall be concerned mainly with questions raised by critical disagreements, particularly about interpretation.

1. '*Hamlet* is a tragedy'. Our first example of a critical judgement is, as criticism, totally banal, and this is true despite the fact that the meaning and application of 'tragedy' have been much debated since Aristotle wrote the *Poetics*. However, we must distinguish between what may now be the uninteresting question, 'Is it a tragedy?', and the deeper one, 'Why is it a tragedy?', i.e. 'Why would those familiar with the play and with the terms say it was so?'. It might be thought that the first question is uninteresting simply because, although various definitions of tragedy have been essayed, *Hamlet* satisfied each definition so well that no-one but a sceptical philosopher could doubt the various judgements that it was a tragedy. But it is not clear that *Hamlet* does satisfy Aristotle's definition.[1] Alternatively, critical boredom may arise from the feeling that though past critics might not have agreed with the contemporary view, their disagreement is not interesting, nor is that of any contemporary Aristotelian.

But why not? 'Such disputes', a modern critic might say, 'are merely about the meanings of a word . . . Our proper interest is in the play.'

But this account of the nature of our non-issue is not so much incorrect as superficial. It is true that if 'tragedy' is defined as Aristotle defined it, *Hamlet*'s claim to be a tragedy may be in question— if, for example, it is not clear that Hamlet is guilty of *hamartia*. Conversely, if a definition of tragedy allows the tragic hero to be guilty of something more than a mere 'mistake', the play's tragic status is not threatened by the flaws and weaknesses in Hamlet's character. But no understanding of this disagreement, and so no understanding of the status of '*Hamlet* is a tragedy', is possible if we treat the verbal disagreement as *just* that. For why have critics come to change their minds about what a tragedy is? And we should remind ourselves that these shifts are brought about by the appearance of new works of art.

What underlies and has given rise to the verbal disagreement is a moral one. Aristotle tells us:

> . . . that the structure of tragedy at its best should be complex, not simple, and that it should represent actions capable of awakening fear and pity— for this a characteristic function of representations of this type. It follows in the first place that good men should not be shown passing from prosperity to misery, for this does not inspire fear or pity, it merely disgusts us. Nor should evil men be shown progressing from misery to prosperity. This is the most untragic of all plots, for it has none of the requisites of tragedy; it does not appeal to our humanity, or awaken pity or fear in us. Nor again should an utterly worthless man be seen falling from prosperity into misery. Such a course might indeed play upon our humane feelings, but it would not arouse either pity or fear; for our pity is awakened by undeserved misfortune, and our fear by that of someone just like ourselves — pity for the undeserving sufferer and fear for the man like ourselves — so that the situation in question would have nothing in it either pitiful or feaful.
>
> There remains a mean between these extremes. This is the sort of man who is not conspicuous for virtue and justice, and whose fall into misery is not due to vice and depravity, but rather to some error, a man who enjoys prosperity and a high reputation . . . [2]

In so doing, he reveals to us, not just an unavoidable lack of knowledge of such plays as *Hamlet*, but a moral harshness and narrowness. It is not just that we would not react as he says men would react to certain dramatic situations, but that we believe that we ought not to do so. The downfall of an evil man could elicit pity and fear, and could properly do so.

Our banal critical judgement, then, which appears merely classificatory, conceals a moral judgement. *Hamlet* is not just adjudged to be a play with certain features of various sorts, but a work that is the proper object of various moral responses.

Having said this we have not exhausted the evaluative dimensions of '*Hamlet* is a tragedy'. For if that *Hamlet* is a proper object of certain moral responses is in some way implied by the judgement that it is a tragedy, then, since it is said to be a play of a certain sort, and since it is a play, it is not sufficient for this judgement that Hamlet himself should have a certain character, or be involved in a certain situation, or that the situation develop in certain ways rather than others, or even that we should have certain moral views about such characters and situations. For *Hamlet* is, in being a play, something which aspires to art, and while all the previous conditions might hold, the play itself might be bad, so bad as to elicit nothing but our boredom or laughter. And if *Hamlet* were grotesquely bad we should hesitate to say that it was a tragedy of any sort, except a failed one. So that in judging that it is a tragedy we commit ourselves not only to certain moral views which would be specified by our account of what is going on in the play and what we mean by 'tragedy', but also to an evaluation that is partly technical of *Hamlet* as a play, *viz.* that at least in some measure it succeeds in portraying persons in situations in a manner that should, and so in appropriate circumstances actually will, move us to what Aristotle described as 'pity and fear'.

The example, then, shows, and shows clearly, that critical judgements can be evaluative in various complex ways even when their surface grammar suggests, and so may mislead us into thinking, that they are merely classificatory and descriptive. We might be particularly tempted to make that mistake in this case because it would provide us with an easy explanation of its banality, *viz.* that *Hamlet* fits well an acceptable definition of 'tragedy' and so is clearly a tragedy, and no-one who knows the play and what the word means can avoid knowing this.

2. '*Hamlet* is a tragedy' raises a further problem. Our acceptance of a definition of tragedy which allows us to count *Hamlet* as one is itself a moral preference. How can such

preferences, which involve commitment to complex claims which the Greeks, perhaps, would scarcely have recognised as moral or even intelligible,[3] be *banal*? It is notorious that substantial evaluative judgements, especially in so far as they are, or involve, moral judgements, are difficult or impossible to establish as true, and so cannot be banal.

What appears to be at least the first step in resolving this problem can be taken by querying the last step in the preceding argument. A judgement is banal, not if it is obviously true, and widely known to be obviously true, and known to be widely known to be obviously true (roughly), but if it is widely held to be true and this is widely believed or known. It is today a banal truth that the earth is round, but it was at one time widely held that the earth was flat and that this was obvious. It was then a banal judgement that the earth was flat.

So '*Hamlet* is a tragedy' may imply various substantial evaluative claims and be banal and yet those implied claims might not be true, or true but not probable, or not easily proved. The problem arises only if we think that what is widely held to be obviously true etc. *is* true, etc. This distinction made, the problem disappears.

But does it? Is the distinction between what is widely held to be obviously true, and what is true, which is so easy to make with regard to the earth's shape, as easy to make when we are dealing with the moral and technical merits of works of art?

Part of our problem may be illuminated by the oblique light cast by the discussion of certain other terms more or less distantly related to 'cathartic', 'moving', etc. Consider, first, 'funny'. What is the connection between something's being funny and its making people laugh? Clearly, something might be funny and yet fail to make a certain group of people laugh; they might be very depressed, or stupid, or frightened. The possible explanations are almost endless. Conversely, something might make a group of people laugh, and laugh spontaneously, and yet it might not be funny *tout court*. It might only be funny to people like them in whatever respect it is that explains why they laugh spontaneously. They may be drunk. But the connection between something's being funny and its making people laugh is not therefore accidental. It is not even or simply causal, or if it were we should have to be able to imagine that what is funny had no tendency to make creatures with a sense of humour laugh. That which is funny, if anything can be described as funny *tout court*, is by definition that which has a tendency or power to make such creatures laugh. So that the possibility of using this term presupposes the existence of a more or less common disposition to respond to certain objects by laughing, smiling etc. And if something *is* funny but does not raise a laugh or smile, this requires explanation.

Of course, since men do have such dispositions, it is not impossible to give very rough accounts of what is funny and what is not that do not mention how men respond to the object in question, but rather features of that object which will produce this response. In a somewhat similar — but not too similar — way, we can discover why things are poisonous, i.e. why their consumption brings about biochemical changes that are unpleasant or fatal, and so construct purely chemical tests for poisons. The tests may indeed be such certain indicators of what they are tests for that it is artificial to regard them as mere signs of the presence of what they test. For example, whether something is sharp depends on its capacity to part substances softer than what it is made of. But its capacity to do that depends on the profile of one of its narrow edges. The dependency is so strong, and we can give such a good explanation of why this is so, that a thing's profile is as much constitutive of its sharpness as whether it cuts or not. Indeed if it did not cut we should try and explain why it did not, without abandoning our view that it was sharp — that indeed is the problem — and if something parted softer substances no matter how thick its blade and how square its edge, we should say that it did so not because it was sharp but for some other reason.

So, returning to 'funny', whether something is indeed funny depends on, is determined by, how people respond — *caeteris paribus*. Now modern comedies, farces, etc. are plays that are intended primarily to make people laugh. So that, provided it is not the case that it is never a virtue in a play to produce that kind of response, if a comedy, a play written with the intention of amusing, does make people laugh, it is to that extent a good comedy and so a good play. The wedge between such a work's being good, and people thinking it good, can only be driven in at all by pointing out that people might be mistaken in thinking that others, or even they themselves, really do laugh at the work in question. We do not have to deny this if it is conceded that whether certain works of art are good — at least in some important dimension — is determined by and depends on what men think about them where the latter is specified by how they tend to respond to them.

We have been trying to establish that the application of the term 'funny', which is a critical term, presupposes certain common responses amongst men; that something is funny if it possesses features that, *caeteris paribus*, will make people laugh; and that, since, as Aristotle would have said, the end of modern comedy is to provoke mirth, the merit of certain works of art, *viz*. comedies, farces, etc., is determined by how audiences tend to respond to them. How men respond in such cases is thus conceptually connected with what is good — unless, again, it is not good that plays should make men laugh. So that if it can be obvious to men that some works of art are funny, and obvious that this is an appropriate, i.e. congruous and intended, response to such works, it is not only obvious, and so banal that such works are good, but *true* that they are good.[4] And how men feel about them, in the sense of responding to them, is not just a *sign* that this is so, but conceptually connected to its being so. The gap between something's being so, and something's being believed to be so, in this way, and to this extent disappears.

However 'funny' is not simply like 'moving' or 'tragic'. For unlike the latter, 'funny' is largely an a-moral term, though we strive sometimes to make it moral. We sometimes say, 'That's not funny', having laughed, not because we think it not funny and others would not laugh, but because we feel we are wrong to laugh. But, even if we are wrong to laugh, if it makes men laugh it *is* funny, even though we feel it ought not to be, and so would not be if we, or men in general, were better than we are.

Getting back to *Hamlet*; we, and Aristotle himself, might find ourselves moved to 'pity and fear' by the play, and yet still, apparently *coherently* doubt that it was truly tragic. For we might agree that we were so moved, though not drunk, or unhappy, and so maudlin, but doubt if our response were morally proper. That is to say, we might be forced to agree that *technically* the play, at least as we saw it produced, was excellent, but feel that we had been seduced, perhaps by that very technical excellence, by the power of the writing and the skill and invention of the production, into an improper feeling of sympathy for the vacillating Hamlet. It would seem, then, that since 'tragic', 'moving', etc. have this important moral dimension, we might agree that any man who was not disabled from responding to the play in the indefinitely large number of ways in which men can be so disabled, might be moved by Hamlet's plight to pity him and fear for men that they might be so placed, and yet still doubt that the play was truly tragic.

Yet, if *this* pervasive response, by men not disabled by drink, unhappiness, their own weaknesses, etc. could not establish that the play was truly tragic, what could? Our being moved to pity and fear by the play does not prove its tragic status, in so far as that proof involves proving that the play embodies deep moral truths, as it does establish its technical excellence; but, though our being moved to pity and fear does not prove its tragic status, what else could? And when we are moved by a tragedy that Aristotle would not have allowed to be tragic — at least, not in the way in which we characteristically see it now as tragic — we feel ourselves more than a mere helpless spectator of our feelings, we feel that it is right and true to respond so.

It will be pointed out that Aristotle and his fellow Greeks might not have been so moved by *Hamlet*. It might also be said that future men, though understanding the play and tutored to an intimate understanding of its archaic English and antique structure, might not share our response either. Surely Aristotle would have abandoned his moral harshness when confronted with *Hamlet*? And if future men could feel nothing for Hamlet, would they not be morally lesser creatures than ourselves? Surely we feel this, and some explanation of why works of art can be felt to so powerfully illuminate moral questions must be ventured.

But could we prove that we are right? *Hamlet*'s implicit claim to certain profound moral truths is not established by how men respond to it, as is its technical excellence. But we must not deny that *Hamlet* and works of a similar structure persuade their audiences that they do establish and reveal moral truths, and if they do not do so, perhaps all talk of truth in moral matters is an illusion.

So this discussion of this example leaves us with two questions. Why do we feel that such works as *Hamlet* can not only present moral claims but establish, if anything can establish, these claims? and are we right in feeling this?

An obvious objection is that if anything can prove their truth, it must be our knowledge and experience of life, and our feelings about that. After all, what happens in a play or novel is determined not by how things are in life, but by the author; and even if he has seen things as they really are, that he has done so can only be determined, not by the work itself, but by its correspondence with life. Moreover, the feeling we sometimes have when we respond to such works, 'How true! That's how it is!' may be engendered not by our suddenly seeing how things are — and how does that happen? — but by the power of the artist, which may depend on the power of his rhetoric, or the beauty of his writing, and not on the accuracy of his perception.

In solving this problem we must deny neither the cogency of these objections nor the strength of our feelings. We have then to find the source of these feelings, and their validity.

Their source is, to some extent, and paradoxically, our knowledge of the areas of life with which the artist is dealing. We may have some vague understanding and awareness of that area from our own experience, but the work of art, if it does arouse our feeling that it has imparted moral truths, has the effect of crystallising this awareness and presenting it to us with a new force and clarity. So what we feel often when we say 'How true! That's how it is!', is simply a recognition of a moral truth of which we had some knowledge; the work of art has served to complete our awareness of it.

But don't we sometimes have a feeling beyond this, that works of art can reveal and establish moral truths in areas of which we have no first-hand, direct knowledge? An explanation of this perhaps is that we draw on our knowledge of other, related areas; and if the work is powerful enough we may need no more than an understanding of what it is to be human to be able to grasp the moral truths it embodies. In addition to this 'connection', where there is no connection the veracity and perception of the work, where it deals with what we do know, permits us to extrapolate to areas where we are unfamiliar or uncertain. We accept, and justifiably accept, the authority of the artist.

If we seem to be claiming here that art can reveal truths to us where life itself cannot, this is not a paradoxical claim. It is not irrational to accept the authority of the artist, if he has established the veracity of his perception in areas where we have some knowledge. This authority is thus sustained even in areas which lie beyond our knowledge of life — in areas where, even if we had had experience of them the truths perceived by the artist would have been beyond our own powers of perception. Often in life our emotions are too closely involved, we are too close to the situation, for us to be able to perceive what is happening to us. A play or novel, on the other hand, though it must involve our emotions if we are to be engaged at all, at the same time keeps us 'at a distance,' by virtue of its being an art object, and therefore something which we approach and to which we are related in a different manner from a live situation.

So the conviction that works of art can present and establish moral truths depends on particular experiences which combine recognition, emotional involvement and personal distance. But this brings us to our second question; i.e. how valid is this conviction, *viz.*, that moral truths can be established by works of art at all? The answer here must be that it is as valid as the feeling that life itself imparts moral truths to us. If we feel and say sincerely that we have grasped such a truth, whether from art or life, how can the validity of our statement be denied? Moral truths are essentially connected with human feelings, and these differ, even among people with similar experience of life, and the moral claims they accept differ. So that, if human nature undergoes a change, only then might the nature of moral truths change. This is not to say, of course, that changes of this kind do not occur; it seems that they do. We are morally different from the Victorians, and our attitude to life and art varies accordingly. The feeling that our attitudes are morally superior might be argued by showing that the Victorians had a much coarser sensibility than ours, that our moral awareness is of a subtler and finer, and therefore better sort. But sometimes this feeling of superiority cannot be argued, though it is none the less real. If we compare ourselves with a past age which made moral distinctions which we do not, these distinctions themselves strike us as unreal or improper, as does, for example, the massive distinction made by the Victorians between male and female adultery. We would still inevitably feel that we had made moral progress, if the disagreement continued, even though we could produce no proof of this beyond the feeling itself.

However, we must not let ourselves be overpersuaded by the feeling that art itself can purvey these truths which thus affect our conduct and our perception of life. For our sense that we have perceived such truths in a work of art might be as transitory as our contact with that work, and might appear unreal, self-indulgent and deceptive, when we are faced with the same or a similar situation in life.

3. 'Shakespeare's sonnet "Let me not to the marriage of true minds" is about the nature of true love.' It is tempting to say that anyone who understands English and who is acquainted with this poem would, in virtue of that general knowledge and his acquaintance with this particular poem, make this judgement and no other.

But a problem remote from the practical critic's problems, and one which is of a philosophical sort, is raised by an indication that this account is inadequate. For although undoubtedly the judgement is correct and is warranted by the poem itself, a reader who understood English might yet fail to make it. A child ignorant of romantic love might not realise what this poem was about; more interestingly, a person from another culture who had learnt our language but was ignorant of the *conventions* of our poetry, ones which might not surround the poetry of his native culture (for example, in this case, that romantic love is a possible topic for poetry) might doubt this; as might a third imagined individual who, for whatever reason, doubts that poetry can be other than oblique.

But since an adult English-speaking occidental could rarely be so ignorant, and therefore could almost as rarely be prey to these doubts, it is very easy to think that the poem will identify what it is about to anyone capable of reading it. And since virtually all criticism is carried on in a context in which the belief that this is so is so natural, general, and well-confirmed that it is scarcely to be described even as an assumption, there is no problem here for the practising critic. Thus what a philosopher milks out of this example has no consequences for our view of what this poem is about, or even — given the critics' characteristic situation— for the basis of this particular judgement, which is the poem. But it is revealing about what must form part of the basis of any judgement, however certain and objective, about what a work of art is about.

Judgements at this level are not incompatible with other, apparently, rival, interpretative claims about the deeper meaning of works, although sometimes there is a temptation to feel an incompatibility here. But, *au pied de la lettre, Animal Farm* is about a group of farmyard animals, including a horse called Boxer and a pig called Major, and one should feel no temptation to deny this just because it is also, and as incontestably, about totalitarianism.

4. What sort of judgement is it, then, that *Animal Farm* is about totalitarianism? A competent reader could not doubt this, and for this very reason it might escape him that there is no literal basis for this judgement in the work. It is then an interpretative judgement the making of which requires something beyond a mere understanding of the language. Yet we would want to say that it is a 'truer' judgement about the work than the previous one, in spite of that's being more literal. The explanation of this last claim is that we know that *Animal Farm* is a sustained allegory, so that its non-literal significance is what is important.

But how do we know that it is a sustained allegory? Again we are asking a question which lies between criticism and philosophy, namely, what is the basis for this claim about *Animal Farm*?

The answer is not an easy one. The undoubted fact that there is such a consistent and striking fit between the surface story — i.e. what happens to the animals in the tale — and what historical evidence shows us about the development of totalitarian states, is both inadequate for the claim's being correct, and over-strong for this. For such a fit may be fortuitous, in which case the work in question may read as an allegory, but is not one.[5] Conversely, a work may be allegorical but a poor allegory precisely because of this lack of fit. Since then a consistent and striking 'fit' is neither sufficient for a work's being allegorical, nor necessary for this, what beyond that 'fit' between the surface story of *Animal Farm* and the development of totalitarian states sustains the irresistible judgement that *Animal Farm* is an allegory about totalitarianism?

The answer must be that this 'fit' is not accidental, which usually means that it is not unintended. But how do we know that it was not unintended? Partly through our knowledge of the time it was written, a time of great political consciousness and awareness of totalitarianism; and partly through our knowledge that the author was himself politically conscious, which we derive from our knowledge of the other works he has written and of the man himself.

The New Critic might now argue against this view that the time the work was written can be established from the text; and that the excellent fit between the surface story and the development of totalitarianism is itself sufficient to establish that this is not accidental. We can concede both these claims without conceding the point that the fit cannot be accidental if this work is indeed an allegory. So in this case we can concede that the text itself may determine that the work is allegorical, without conceding the New Critic's thesis that the truth of this judgement does not depend on the truth of claims about what the author intended, or when it was written. The New Critic or indeed any critic who feels his proper concern to be the text, may now concede that his interpretation of a work does involve references to what the author intended, and hence to the time at which the work was written; but only in so far as those intentions are realised in the work itself.

But the artificiality of this position is made clear when we imagine that the moral certainties which he derives from the text of *Animal Farm* and which in turn sustain his view of when it was written and why, are false, or let him down. Suppose we make the almost unbelievable, but logically possible, supposition that Stalin himself wrote this work. Would not what we know about Stalin, independently of his having written *Animal Farm*, have consequences for our reading of this work? Our prior and morally certain view of what intentions are realised in the text would here conflict with our certainties about Stalin which we derive from elsewhere. What the critic with his concern for the text may say at this point, is, 'No; the text alone determines our interpretation or reading of a work, and in this case it would demonstrate that Stalin was no Stalinist'. But surely this is much too strong? Surely the most we could say, and would say, is that we don't know what to make of Stalin's views, because there is this conflict between what we know about him, and *Animal Farm*. And what else we know about him sends us back to the text looking for — and who would say that we should not find — ambiguities of meaning that we had not previously noted (and which indeed would not have existed if we had assumed Orwell's authorship).

Alternatively, a critic, conceding that the imaginary authorship might have consequences for our interpretation of *Animal Farm*, might take the equally heroic line that therefore the text is ambiguous, that it does not fully realise the intention to write a work condemning totalitarianism. But this is to abandon his earlier interpretation of the text, and for reasons that lie beyond the text. It is also to abandon the claim, which is a correct and incontrovertible one, that *Animal Farm* is indeed a sustained allegory about, and condemning, totalitarianism.

So again, what we milk from this example, which is critically uncontroversial, is something which could have no consequences for the critic making particular judgements. But it

helps us to a realisation of what underpins such critical judgements; and though the theoretical critic, interested in the basis
for such judgements, may accept what we say as obvious, he
may also do this without realising that it is contrary to a
theoretical stance he sometimes takes, e.g. the stance that all
our judgements about a work must come from 'within' the
work itself.

5. It is even harder to uncover and understand the basis of
judgements made about a work written and readable on two
levels where there is no simple correspondence between the
surface story and the deeper level of meaning. As we noticed
earlier, in some such cases where there is not a consistent and
striking 'fit' we might simply be dealing with a poorly written
allegory. But in other cases, the allegory might be well-written
and undoubtedly valuable, but it may raise insurmountable
difficulties in determining the significance of its deeper level of
meaning.

Gulliver's Travels is a case of this kind. We want to say that
this is undoubtedly a work written and readable on two levels,
the deeper of which is concerned with man's moral state and is
of the greater significance. The text itself demands such a
reading, and our knowledge of Jonathan Swift can only serve
to corroborate and strengthen this reading.

But the critic will then ask, 'What is the precise nature of the
deeper significance?' and with *Gulliver's Travels* he is in a far
more difficult position for answering that question than he is
with *Animal Farm*. The Houyhnhnms lie at the heart of the
problem. The Houyhnhnms clearly stand in some symbolic
relation to man's moral state — but what is the exact nature of
that relation? It can be argued, and was once commonly
thought, that they represented Swift's view of moral perfection, and that they successfully did this. Or alternatively, they
might be intended to represent moral perfection, but this
intention is imperfectly realised. A third possibility is that they
are the successful realisation of Swift's intention to represent
the impossibility of moral perfection. The first two interpretations differ only in relation to how successful Swift was; but
they both differ radically from the third in their view of what is

intended. The text is elusive enough to allow for the possibility of both views of what is intended, so that neither can be shown to be the correct one in terms of the text.

When critics ask what precisely *Gulliver's Travels* is about, are they asking what interpretation of the text, elicited from the text, is the correct one? If so, the question is unanswerable. The doubt this raises about the nature of critical activity can, however, be satisfactorily settled by the explanation any modern critic might give, that he does not expect to discover the 'correct' interpretation, if indeed that exists; but that the very business of pursuing the question of what this work is about will illuminate the work and help us to a better understanding of it.

But because this is a case where the text is elusive, in a way in which *Animal Farm* is not, the critic might think that here external information might help him to discover the 'correct' interpretation. Could any such information help him to do so?

Suppose that the critic found a journal of Swift's including a statement that the idea of moral perfection was an impossible one. He might then see this statement as corroborating the view he had tentatively held (but for which the text provided less than proof), that the work was about the impossibility of man's achieving moral perfection, and that the Houyhnhnms were the embodiment of that impossibility. The purist might present the objection here that, though the elusiveness of what the Houyhnhnms represented was a feature of the text, there was no way that it could be shown from the text that this was *intended* to be the case, so that there was no support in the text for the critic's view, and his external evidence must be inadmissible without such support. But here the critic concerned only with the text seems to be leaning over backwards to maintain his theoretical position, since the only way the text itself could establish the correctness of either of the rival interpretations here would be its containing a statement of what is intended, i.e. a statement within the text which explicitly determines its own interpretation. But don't even statements of this sort require interpretation? May they not, for example, be intended ironically?

So this is the sort of case where external evidence could

properly be used to strengthen an interpretation, where this interpretation could not be so firmly established from the text alone. The purist's position does reveal, however, that it could not establish that this was the only possible interpretation. For it could still be argued, by someone who had been persuaded by the text that the Houyhnhnms did embody moral perfection, that Swift had succeeded in portraying this, despite his beliefs to the contrary. We can concede him this, while insisting that the external evidence strengthens the rival interpretation.

What we have been discussing is an extreme case, and that is its interest. But there are cases where, if we are to understand the work in question, and appreciate it fully, we can only do so with the help of external information. Many critics hold the view that only the text is the proper object of critical concern, and they appear to think that the text is only what it physically is — the marks on the page. This view is never correct, but its absurdity is fully revealed in cases where information which requires more than a knowledge of the language in which the work is written, is essential to our understanding and appreciation. This information might be about the significance of a name (how could we understand Sylvia Plath's 'Ariel' if we did not know that that was the name of a horse?), or about the author (the irony of Swift's 'Modest Proposal' is balanced finely enough to deceive some readers into taking it straight, if they did not know its author, or the significance of that knowledge), or about a convention which has not survived to our times (Elizabethan lyrics would strike us as absurd if we were not familiar with the courtly love convention). Whatever the nature of the information, if it seems to help us to understand or appreciate a work more fully, it will be seen as a part of the work which it is as proper to consider as the text itself.

There is a danger here, too, of course; we must not concentrate on such information at the expense of the text, just as we must not concentrate on the text at the expense of the helpful material which might surround it. For example, if we were to read *Sons and Lovers* with one eye constantly on its relation to D.H. Lawrence's own life, we might be led away from the significance which the novel imparts on its own account. So we must learn to consider each work as a separate case, and use our intelligence and sensitivity to judge how much we should include as part of the work, and how much of what is available to us in connection with a text we should regard as the proper object of our critical concern. Only in this way can we avoid the temptation, so great in criticism, to take a monolithic line.

Works of art, created as they are by men, are after all historical objects, and that being so, our aesthetic responses to them have to be responses to them as that. If we don't admit this, we find ourselves having to deny what cannot be denied — that, for example, imitative works are less than what they imitate, or even aesthetically, quite different from what they imitate, although physically very like their models. Tudor houses are not twee, but a modern imitation can scarcely avoid this. The landscape 'Cavalcade by the Seashore', an illustration in *The Turin Hours* attributed to Hubert Van Eyck, looks almost Victorian, but this fact, far from reducing it to the status of Victorian landscapes, only heightens the wonder of it.

6. '*Hamlet* is a tragedy about revenge'. This might be a judgement about what, literally, *Hamlet* is about[6] and as such it is unarguable and banal — and for that reason uninteresting and rarely made. But it might *also* be an interpretative judgement about what the play is centrally concerned with, or concerned with on a deeper level (cf. '*Animal Farm* is about totalitarianism'); and our view of the truth of this judgement is one which can and indeed has changed with the passing of time, and the accompanying change in our knowledge and sensibility.

In the early seventeenth century the interpretative judgement would have been as banal as the one about the play's literal meaning; revenge was one of the central, popular themes of the time.[7] But revenge no longer exercises us practically or — perhaps therefore — imaginatively; in those ways it is no longer a part of our lives, and so we no longer regard it as one of the deep concerns of tragedy. Indeed Shakespeare's own work has revealed to us more lasting universal themes.

There are two possible objections to this view of the change in the nature of the interpretative judgement. A critic might feel that the interpretative judgement is as incontestable as the

verbally indistinguishable judgement about the literal meaning of the play, not because he has not made the distinction
between them, but because he believes, on historical, scholarly
grounds, that if the latter is true the former must be true.[8] As
the Elizabethans could properly derive the incontestable truth
of the interpretative judgement from the incontestable truth of
the literal judgement, so it must be today. But such a critic
ignores a crucial fact. We are not Elizabethans; our conventions, our social and cultural climate, our sensibility, have all
changed with the passing of time. For us the interpretative
claim is no longer undeniable.

Another critic might admit that revenge is no longer part of
our lives and that for this reason most of the plays which have
revenge as their deep concern are limited (hence the somewhat
derogatory note in the description 'revenge tragedy'), whilst
arguing that *Hamlet* transcends these local limitations and
makes revenge a living theme again. But surely by the very fact
of its transcending its local limitations, the theme would be
inescapably transformed? It might plausibly be argued that
revenge can be seen as the play's deep concern, but it would
not be so in the way that it was for the Elizabethans.

The claim that *Hamlet* is a tragedy about revenge is now one
of many interpretative claims about the play, a further example of which we discuss next.

7. '*Hamlet* is a Christian tragedy.' This is exactly the same kind
of judgement as the previous example, in that it is interpretative, but here it is much clearer that it is that sort of claim, and
also clearer that it is contestable.

Nevertheless, the critic who makes it may feel that, as in the
example previously discussed, there is a literal basis in the text
for his judgement, if one looks at the text in the right way, and
he may be right. But how does he come to prefer this interpretative judgement to others which also have a literal basis in
the text? D.G. Allen[9] wants to say that the view that *Hamlet* is
a Christian tragedy, although it is not the only view of the play
that can be taken, is the most comprehensive, consistent view
in terms of the evidence in the play, and he therefore claims it
as the 'truest' view.

Can any sense be given to this claim? Some interpretations would be wrong. But is there any difference between the status of this judgement and that of, say, '*Hamlet* is a tragedy about man's search for identity', or '*Hamlet* portrays the tragic struggle to preserve a moral position in the midst of corruption'? Allen would want to say that the latter judgements are not wrong, not inconsistent with the play, but are more highly interpretative, for there is less support for them in the play itself, and that they spring from a sense of aesthetic dissatisfaction left by the more accurate, consistent interpretation.

But this last point raises questions, not about the differences, or indeed the confusions, between interpretative and literal judgements, but rather questions about the status of interpretative judgements. Allen's argument seems a curious one to use to support the correctness of his interpretation. He seems to elevate certain critical principles to a level where they must determine our considered view of a work, regardless of our response to that work. But if an interpretation does not satisfy us aesthetically, if it leaves a gap between the view it provides of the work and our response to that work — and Allen freely admits that his interpretation may be of this kind — must there not be something lacking in the interpretation, however well-founded it may be in terms of the critical principles? Doesn't our sense of aesthetic dissatisfaction reveal that the principles alone are not reliable in a case like this? Allen's scholarly principles are not improper or irrelevant, but what does seem improper is his argument that principles like this should *always* control our response. Of course, principles do sometimes determine our response, or cause us to modify it retrospectively. But this is no objection to our point here, which is that when our informed response *remains* in conflict with our principles, it is the principles we must abandon, at least in this sort of case. To stick to them would lead us, as it leads Allen, to view the proliferation of critical interpretations of a work like *Hamlet* as a sign of something wrong either with the work or with the critics, if not both; whereas this proliferation may be seen more appropriately as a sign of richness in the work to aspects of which critics severally respond.

Most critics would want to argue that there is a stronger connection between principles and response than this case seems to reveal, and would see critical principles as central in making and justifying their judgements. In the examples which follow, we shall look at some further cases of critical disagreement and examine this and other questions about the nature and validity of the statements critics make, questions which are highlighted when these statements seem to conflict with each other.

8. 'The mood of "My Papa's Waltz"[10] is one of excitement and exuberance.' This judgement may be seen as incontrovertible on our first reading of the poem, though the very word 'mood' warns us that it is interpretative, or at least not determined solely by the literal meaning of the words in the poem (though of course it is determined to some extent by that; the literal meaning rules out some interpretations). But suppose that we are presented with another, apparently contrary judgement; 'The mood of "My Papa's Waltz" is one of fear and tension.' Now, perhaps surprisingly, both claims are consistent with the literal meaning of the sequence of lines which constitute the poem. This sort of ambiguity is usually restricted to single sentences, cf. 'Shut the door'. With this sort of sentence, the context, and tone of voice if it is spoken, can help us to decide whether it is a request or a command. However, in the case of the poem, context and tone of voice cannot help to resolve the issue, because they are not there. So which view of the poem, if either, is right?

It might seem helpful in trying to sort out what does, or should, decide a disagreement of this sort to consider the different ways in which we might interpret, or misinterpret, a man's smile, and how we decide who is right here. If a man is grinning broadly, and his eyes are shining, we might say with some certainty that he is feeling happy or excited. And we would say confidently not just that he looked happy but that he *was* happy, because his expression was the expression characteristically worn by happy people. But someone else might see a darker side to the man's smile — suggestions of strain, or perhaps a sinister gleam, in the eyes. The expression could then give us no help in deciding which view was right, for it provides support for both views. And which view we would take might depend on our own mood or on the situation in which we saw the man in question. Exactly the same is true of the poem; indeed it would be possible for us to hold one interpretation at one time and the opposite at another (cf. Köhler's well-known duck-rabbit drawing).

Often, however, in such a case, a reader will resist a new interpretation, perhaps because the first interpretation has become so familiar that it is impossible for him to see the poem in any other way. Or he may resist it because he falsely believes that it is not possible for the literal sense to support two apparently opposing interpretations. But there is yet another sort of case where he will resist the new interpretation, even while admitting that it is consistent with the literal sense of the lines, for other, and proper, reasons. For example, one might have to admit that a view of John Donne's 'Valediction: forbidding mourning' which sees the tone as ironic and insincere is, strictly, consistent with the sense of the lines, but one can properly argue that such a view is nevertheless perverse, diminishes the poem, and is inconsistent with what we know of much of Donne's other work and character (and particularly of the other Valedictions). Disagreement, and argument, over such a case would not be pointless (though it might not lead to any resolution).

But to return to the case of 'My Papa's Waltz'; here it is quite possible for the 'sensitive' reader to see both aspects of the poem, even at once,[11] to see it as combining fear and excitement, tension and happiness; and perhaps this would be the only complete view of the poem.

At this point our analogy breaks down. For whether the man's smile really does express happiness or strain is in principle determinable, and depends on the man's state of mind. We could discover which was the correct interpretation of his smile by asking him how he felt at the time (assuming his reply to be sincere), or by learning more about his situation. Of course, there is normally a strong correlation between a man's inner feelings and his outward expression; if there were not, we could not even recognise an expression characteristic of feelings of happiness, for there would be no such thing. And if there seemed to be a great disparity between a man's feelings and his expression, we might be unable to see his expression as *expressive* of his feelings. Thus we might still want to say that his smile 'looked strained' — but this would no longer be an interpretative claim, merely a description of the appearance of his facial expression.

There is nothing analogous to this test in the case of the poem. It might be argued here, likewise, that the 'state of mind' of the poet, or more plausibly, what he intended, might stand in the same relation to the poem. But while there are undoubtedly cases of poems and other works of art where our knowledge of the author and the circumstances in which he produced the work will have consequences for the way we interpret the work[12], there are others in which some of us will be affected by this information and others not;[13] and still others where the ambiguity of tone will not be removed for most of us by this information.[14] Sometimes the ambiguity of tone in a work may strike us as so patent — even though we may have had to have it pointed out to us initially — that we may regard it as a better indicator of what the artist really felt or intended than anything else we might know about him or that he might say. (The same is true of certain ambiguous remarks.)

The difference, then, between smiles and works of art is this. The significance of a smile depends on the natural connection which exists between it and the state of mind of the person on whose face it is seen. An interpretation of a smile is therefore a more or less well-founded inference about the state of mind of that person. But the significance of a work of art, whether poem, painting or piece of music, resides within the work itself, and an interpretation of it is an attempt to understand that significance, and not the significance of anything beyond it. And though a work of art is a function of its author, and therefore its significance is determined to some extent by the identity of that author, the circumstances in which it was written etc., nevertheless these are only some amongst the many completely related factors which determine the significance of a work of art.

Works of art should not — indeed, cannot — be simply seen

or primarily seen as guides to the state of mind of the author. Even if Roethke told us what mood he had intended to convey in this poem, although this might influence the way we read the poem, it could not determine which of these judgements was the right one, for this is a case where the ambiguity of tone, once it is pointed out to us, is hard to ignore, and it indicates more strongly than any other information we might have that there is no one 'right' reading of this poem.

The critics' judgements in this case, then, are not simply incompatible though the critics who pass them will probably believe them to be so, for they are made by persons who see different aspects of the poem, and either can be seen, depending on how we look at the poem. It would be a mistake therefore for either critic to try to argue that his was the 'right' view. All a critic should do in a case of this kind is put his point of view in such a way that it enables the reader to see this aspect of the poem.

The rival interpretations of Roethke's poem are both consistent with the literal meaning of its text, and it is this which explains why the poem can be seen and read in either way. But consistency with the literal meaning or meanings of the text of a poem is not in all cases sufficient to ensure that an interpretation is tenable, as we shall try to show with the following example.

9. The images suggested by 'instant fires', 'birds of prey' and 'at once our time devour', implying a positive attack upon sensual pleasures, is followed by two images which (despite obscurities) evoke both the harmony and physical violence of sexual love:

> Let us roll all our strength, and all
> Our sweetness, up into one ball:
> And tear our pleasures with rough strife,
> Thorough the Iron Gates of life.

The strength of the man and the sweetness of the woman are now united in a sexual embrace (the 'ball' may be pomander, or Plato's original Hermaphrodite — or just a ball). The second image is a complicated conceit describing the physical experience of love, in which the geography of the woman's body is alluded to by reference to the Danubian Iron Gates. (Lovelace uses the expression 'rosy gates' in a sexual sense.)

Many poets have advised us to enjoy life while we may in tones which range from gay hedonism to what seems rather like compulsive desperation. Marvell's poem combines many moods: the ironical, almost detached, pose of the first section changes abruptly to a controlled appreciation of death's sinister but ingenious mockery of human behaviour. The final section betrays, by its imagery, a certain aggressive satisfaction in 'devouring' time and 'tearing' pleasures, so that one feels that Marvell's conquest of time and death by love is no mere verbal victory, but rather the reflection of a powerful, emotional desire to live intensely:

> Thus, though we cannot make our sun
> Stand still, yet we will make him run.

D. Davison, *The Poetry of Andrew Marvell* (London, 1964), p. 27

But then, what are we to say about Marvell's famous

> Let us roll all our strength and all
> Our sweetness up into one ball:
> And tear our pleasures with rough strife,
> Thorough the Iron Gates of life?

We have always accepted these lines. Yet there is surely something very odd about the image: if I try to visualize it, I see nothing but two lovers feverishly trying to squeeze an india-rubber ball through the bars of an iron gate . . . Marvell's metaphors of 'ball' & 'gates' are relatively abstract, carrying no colour or detail which could force itself upon our senses. So we may say, provisionally, that mixed metaphors or incongruous images seem to be successful in proportion as they lack sensuous appeal. Secondly, there is the question of emotional propriety. The two metaphors in the Marvell image perfectly express the emotional violence of his theme at this point: and, just because there is such human passion there, a poetic passion can be generated which fuses the ideas of ball and iron gate . . . Lastly, there is the matter of context. Times without number, if we closely examine the context of some mixed metaphor or apparently arbitrary image which has nevertheless won our imaginative assent, we find that our minds have already to some extent been prepared for it. The lines preceding that Marvell quotation run as follows –

> Now let us sport us while we may;
> And now, like amorous birds of prey,
> Rather at once our time devour
> Than languish in his slow-chapt power.

I fancy that the word 'sport', and the hint of imprisonment in the last line, which may well have suggested to the poet the subsequent metaphors of 'ball' and 'iron gates', do prepare the reader's mind to accept these metaphors, violently contrasted though they are, by pre-establishing a delicate link between them.

C. Day Lewis, *The Poetic Image* (London, 1947),
pp. 72–4.

We wish to argue that Davison gives a more correct reading of Marvell's lines than Day Lewis. However, our primary concern is not critical but metacritical: on what grounds do we make this judgement? Or are we merely responding to the more powerful critical rhetoric?

The critics differ in the metaphorical meanings which they find in the lines. Now it might be said in Day Lewis' favour that his is at once the less vulgar and the more careful interpretation. His quest for the possible meanings within the image is extensive, just because he finds himself puzzled by the disparity between the oddness of what he sees as a mixed metaphor, and the fact that nonetheless we give it our imaginative assent! He realises, too, the importance of other factors such as the context of the lines in deciding what they may be trying to convey.

Yet, for all his care, Lewis is blind— aspect-blind, one might say — to what would seem to be an obvious feature of the metaphor, its sexual significance.

But is it obvious? We feel it to be so because the sexual connotations of 'sweetness', 'ball'[15] 'tear', 'gates' ('iron' because the lady is a virgin?), which Lewis presumably does not see, are strongly suggested not just by the fact that the words occur in a poem which is amongst other things an essay in seduction, of which the lines in question are the climax, but also by the explicit sexual sense of the lines immediately preceding these, which Davison spells out. For Lewis, unless he is being extremely coy, the link forged between 'sport' and 'ball' is of the playing-field variety. And whilst he sees the imprisonment link between Time's 'slow-chapt power' and 'iron gates', he fails to understand its ironic substance: the lady herself condemns them to the prison of Time by locking up herself against her lover. Thus, though Lewis must be intellectually aware of the sexual context of these lines, he seems not to feel its force; no one who did could visualise this image so improbably as 'two lovers feverishly trying to squeeze an india rubber ball through the bars of an iron gate''[16].

But there is a possible objection on Lewis' behalf here: can the presence of mere connotations be clearly established? And can we not find sexual connotations anywhere if we try hard enough? Certainly, there will be cases where it will be more difficult than it is here to decide whether connotations are present and relevant; and we encounter a similar problem with what might be called implications (though these can be as central and as clearly felt as the literal meanings of words, cf. 'I gave commands; Then all smiles stopped together' in Browning's 'My Last Duchess').[17] Indeed, if we needed further confirming evidence in this case, Davison provides it, referring to a generally recognised source of the physiological significance of 'iron gates' and to another poet's exploitation of this significance.

Yet our view that Lewis is wrong springs from what is both less and more than such evidence; a knowledge of, or at any rate a moral certainty about, how men characteristically behave and how their minds work. Marvell expresses man's desperate desire to attack life, live it to the full, through the sweeter 'attack' of making love, and we feel that most men will naturally understand both that feeling, and the sexual metaphor in which Marvell expresses it. Davison's professional recognition and account of this simply makes complete and public what most of us have thought, some of us perhaps self-doubtingly, in private, and transforms these separate views into a communion of thought.

The last example has shown that an interpretation's consistency with the literal meaning of a text is not sufficient for our regarding it as acceptable. Among the many points that we wish to make in our discussion of the next example is that consistency with the literal meaning of the text may not even be necessary, in rare cases, for our regarding it as tenable, or as good.

10. Confronted suddenly with the active physical beauty of the bird, he conceives it as the opposite of his patient spiritual renunciation; the statements of the poem appear to insist that his own life is superior, but he cannot decisively judge between them, and holds both with agony in his mind. *My*

heart in hiding would seem to imply that the *more dangerous* life is that of the Windhover, but the last three lines insist it is *no wonder* that the life of renunciation should be the more *lovely*. *Buckle* admits of two tenses and two meanings: 'they do buckle here,' or 'come, and buckle yourself here'; *buckle* like a military belt, for the discipline of heroic action, and *buckle* like a bicycle wheel, 'make useless, distorted, and incapable of its natural motion.' *Here* may mean 'in the case of the bird,' or 'in the case of the Jesuit'; *then* 'when you have become like the bird,' or 'when you have become like the Jesuit.' *Chevalier* personifies either physical or spiritual activity; Christ riding to Jerusalem, or the cavalryman ready for the charge; Pegasus, or the Windhover.

Thus in the first three lines of the sestet we seem to have a clear case of the Freudian use of opposites, where two things thought of as incompatible, but desired intensely by different systems of judgments, are spoken of simultaneously by words applying to both; both desires are thus given a transient and exhausting satisfaction, and the two systems of judgment are forced into open conflict before the reader. Such a process, one might imagine, could pierce to regions that underlie the whole structure of our thought; could tap the energies of the very depths of the mind. At the same time one may doubt whether it is most effective to do it so crudely as in these three lines; this enormous conjunction, standing as it were for the point of friction between the two worlds conceived together, affects one rather like shouting in an actor, and probably to many readers the lines seem so meaningless as to have no effect at all. The last three lines, which profess to come to a single judgment on the matter, convey the conflict more strongly and more beautifully.

William Empson, *Seven Types of Ambiguity*
(2nd ed., 1961), pp. 225–6

From the opening 'I caught this morning morning's minion' to 'the achieve of, the mastery of the thing' the poet is in an ecstasy of amazement at the mastery and brilliant success of the windhover — a beauty so great that it is difficult to imagine any that has its equal.

But there is a beauty far, far greater. And the sestet is devoted to a revelation of a beauty beyond this beauty, a beauty which is 'a billion times told lovelier, more dangerous' than the purely natural and triumphant flight. And whence comes this achievement which is more than achievement, this mastery which is more than mastery?

It is in the act of 'buckling', when the windhover swoops down, when its flight is crumpled, when 'brute beauty and valour and act, oh, air, pride, plume' in an act of self-sacrifice, of self-destruction, of mystical self-immolation send off a fire far greater than any natural beauty:

> Brute beauty and valour and act, oh, air, pride, plume, here
> Buckle! And the fire that breaks from thee then, a billion
> Times told lovelier, more dangerous, O my chevalier!

Nor is this to be wondered at, for this is true even in humble little things — is true of everything: the sheen of common earth shines out when the plough breaks it into furrows; and fire breaks from fire only in the moment of its own destruction:

> No wonder of it: shéer plód makes plough down sillion
> Shine, and blue-bleak embers, ah my dear,
> Fall, gall themselves, and gash gold-vermilion.

Here is Christ upon the Cross and Hopkins the *alter Christus*. Beautiful was Christ's public life, but 'a billion times told lovelier' was His self-immolation on the Cross, His sacrifice transmuted by the Fire of Love into something far greater than any more natural beauty.

J. Pick, *Gerard Manley Hopkins, Priest and Poet*
(London, 1942), p. 71

Hopkins' poem has attracted myriad critical accounts, and this, along with the opacity and ambiguity which are responsible for it, makes the question of which account is right a particularly exercising one. Here, again, we want to argue that one of our quoted critics, Empson, gives a more correct account; but again our interest is metacritical, and we shall try to show that Pick's misreading is produced in part by his desire to attain one of the proper goals of criticism.

At the heart of Pick's account is the assertion that in the act of buckling, the bird's stoop on its prey, the windhover is performing an act of 'self-destruction, of mystical self-immolation' which he sees as parallel with Christ's supreme act of sacrifice, and with the poet's own lesser self-sacrifice in the service of Christ. Pick, himself a widely acknowledged Hopkins scholar, is not alone in this view; R.V. Schoder describes the bird's 'perilous, triumphant activity, the reckless abandon to the nobility of the deed in forgetfulness of all toil and pain to self '[18] and Romano Guardini argues 'However the word "buckle" may be explicated, it includes the meaning that what was before free in the heights, surrounded by light, unlimited . . . must now yield to or become a thing that dwells in the lower darkness, constricted, care-worn, yet in truth, greater'.[19]

Pick and his fellow-critics seem unaware that the wind-hover's supposed act of 'self-immolation' is in fact an act of self-preservation, of destruction not of itself but of another, weaker, of God's creatures. Indeed, they seem unaware that the windhover is a bird of prey at all — as do all those critics who see the windhover unproblematically as an analogue of Christ (though not necessarily of his self-sacrifice)[20] otherwise they would surely feel the moral strain there. That analogue is, of course, suggested by the dedication or address of the poem 'To Christ our Lord', and also by the associations of certain words like 'dauphin' and 'chevalier'. One wonders whether critics can more easily ignore the incongruity of the analogue because of the beauty of the word 'windhover', which describes the bird's flight and nothing else.

But this cannot be the only explanation of their, and especially Pick's, lack of awareness. Part of the explanation may lie in the fact that a major interpretative difficulty is presented by the transition from the mood of joy and triumph in the octet to the much more muted, resigned mood in the sestet, a transition contained in a particularly obscure tercet. Now what is for the most part a proper expectation that what a poet writes (and especially one as conscious of language as Hopkins) will make sense,[21] will put pressure on a critic always to find a coherent interpretation, even in those rare cases where there *is* incoherence in the work. Pick's interpretation makes convenient sense of Hopkins' obscure transition.

But why this particular, perverse sense? The explanation for this lies in Hopkins' peculiar status as a priest and poet. A high proportion of the critics who discuss his work are themselves priests, or of a religious persuasion, and this results in a strong pressure to find interpretations of Hopkins' poems which reveal him as totally devoted to his calling.[22] Pick demolishes any suggestion of Hopkins' doubting his own self-sacrifice in this poem, by the happy stroke of seeing the prime, powerful figure in the poem as a symbol of self-sacrifice.

We have, then, at least a partial explanation of the perversity of some interpretations of 'The Windhover'. But is an interpretation which is inconsistent at some point with the literal sense of a work necessarily wrong? It may not be, where there is an inconsistency within the work (e.g. Natasha in *War and Peace* is described as 13 in 1805, 15 in 1806, and 16 in 1809) and a critic deliberately ignores this in his account on the grounds that the inconsistency is accidental, and peripheral. He will at best relegate this to a footnote in talking about Natasha's development. Indeed, this selection by omission goes on before the 'critical' stage is ever reached: an editor who discovers what seems to be a simple error in a manuscript — a misspelling, the same word repeated consecutively, perhaps even, in what is likely to be a corrupt text, a character twice entering the scene in a play with no intervening exit — will correct the error, his overall view of the work will determine his reading even though this goes against the literal sense.

We may be similarly sympathetic to a reading which overlooks an actual incoherence in a work, if this were simply a grammatical incoherence and the report of the line or lines was quite clear. Or a critic might provide a possible 'solution' to an incoherence which had previously puzzled us,[23] though here we might be happier to accept the solution if the incoherence were minor, and the line or lines of peripheral importance in the work.

But of course whether a feature is peripheral, and indeed whether it is intended, and whether this is relevant, are themselves interpretative questions about which we may sometimes differ.[24]

There are cases, then, where an interpretation inconsistent with the literal meaning may nonetheless be acceptable, though determining whether we have a case of that kind can itself be problematic. Not so, however, in the case under discussion. Pick not only ignores a major characteristic of the central figure in the poem; he makes that omission the keystone of his interpretation. Furthermore, there are, *pace* Yvor Winters,[25] coherent interpretations of the poem which are not erroneous, and spring from an awareness of the incongruity between the poem's physical subject and its spiritual undertow. Empson's is one such, and we hope it speaks for itself; another is that it is the bird's beauty which 'buckles', i.e. collapses, thus making the poet more aware of the beauties of the spiritual life.[26] These readings in their different ways make clear how unnecessary is the sort of perversity we find in Pick's account.

Empson's is a fuller reading, and one which makes for a richer poem. But it should be noted that these are not our grounds for arguing that his reading is to be preferred to Pick's. They are instead that the poem warrants such a reading, and does not warrant Pick's. But it is no accident that what is warranted generally — and in this case — produces a better reading than one which is not warranted, or one which is inadequate. Poetry is not usually improved by accident, which in turn reinforces our view that Empson's reading is warranted.

Now fuller readings, even when they produce richer and better poems, are not always warranted, i.e. as interpretations of what the poet wrote; they are not when, for example, we know that he cannot have intended, or be construed as having written, the fuller, richer work. Such interpretations produce better poems, but they literally do produce them. This is no absolute objection to creative interpretation, but creative interpretation should be seen for what it is. Nor should it be assumed that the richer, fuller reading always produces the better poem; sometimes it can lead to a richness of meaning that is indigestible as well as unwarranted.

We have tended, in the above, to make what is today a common assumption, *viz.*, that richness and ambiguity, while they can be overdone, are *desiderata,* and this assumption can only guide our reading of poetry written by poets who share that assumption, but misguide our reading of the work of writers of other periods who did not. The fact that this poem has attracted such a wealth of critical attention no doubt has a simple connection with the poem's merit. But complexity and opacity do provide the critic with endless opportunities for his art, and sometimes a poem which is simple will attract less attention than an inferior poem which is complex, just in virtue of that.

The role of 'literal sense' in resolving the kinds of disagreement we have been considering is perhaps more variable than one might expect. But there are certain cases of disagreement where it can play no useful role at all. In our final example in this chapter we consider the difficulties raised by such a case.

11. In personal relations with Skrebensky, however, she manifests an inadequacy answering to his. The essential relation between them is given in their dancing, as they dance together at Frederick Brangwen's wedding supper, which is also a celebration of harvest; the whole thing — the supper, the dance, and the subsequent scene in the moonlit stackyard — being done with a sensuous, disturbing force that is intensely Lawrence.

> F.R. Leavis on Ursula, *D.H. Lawrence: Novelist* (London, 1955), p. 140.

Hence the strangeness of his novels; and hence also, it must be admitted, certain qualities of violent monotony, and intense indistinctness, qualities which make some of them for all their richness and their unexpected beauty, so curiously difficult to get through . . . I have known readers whose reaction to Lawrence's books was very much the same as Lawrence's own reaction to the theory of evolution. What he wrote meant nothing to them because they 'did not feel it *here*' — in the solar plexus.

> A. Huxley, *The Achievement of D.H. Lawrence*, ed. Hoffman and Moore (Oklahoma, 1953), p. 63.

Lawrence is perhaps the classic writer who has attracted more critical disagreement than any other, and disagreement of a sort very difficult to resolve. For the disagreement is often at heart a moral one, and though voiced and located in terms of the work, it cannot be settled by reference to the text, for critics may agree about what is there, but disagree in their evaluation of it.

Thus Leavis constructs careful arguments directed at explaining the power of Lawrence's writing; whilst a reader of Huxley's disposition,[27] who does not 'feel it here' when reading the passage to which Leavis refers might, in justification of this, argue that the language was for him strained and unnatural, typical of the sort of jargon Lawrence falls back on when trying to express intense inner feelings. He might also say that the scene was invested with no symbolic significance for him, and therefore he found the passage eventually repetitive and strained.

How are we to decide between Leavis' account of this passage, and that of our hypothetical critic? Both see exactly the same words, possibly even the same aim on the part of the writer, but for one it is rich and pleasing, while for the other it fails and is strained and uninteresting. Reference to principles will not help for reasons we have discussed earlier, and in any case, either critic might well argue that Lawrence is an exception to any principles, because he is trying to do something no other writer has ever attempted. Nor is this a case like the disagreement over 'My Papa's Waltz', where the critics were presenting different interpretations, views of different aspects of the same work which were both sustained by the work and so were not incompatible. In the Lawrence case, the critics' accounts are incompatible, because even though they agree on their interpretation of the work, they differ on their evaluation of it.

This is not a case, either, where the text can provide us with evidence that one account is better than another; it is not a matter simply of close reading. In fact, either critic might well appeal to the same words in the text to support his view, because each one has a different evaluative response to the text (i.e. they might agree exactly on their view of *what* Lawrence was trying to say and do, but one might point to it and say, 'Look how terrible this is', while the other might point to the very same thing and say 'Look how marvellous this is'). Nor do the participants in this dispute think that the text needs to be amplified, or that we need more information about Lawrence and his situation, to see and understand it properly. They agree about what is there in the work; where they disagree is on the value of what is there. We are reminded of C.S. Lewis' comment on his disagreement with Leavis over *Paradise Lost*:

It is not that he and I see different things when we look at *Paradise Lost*. He sees and hates the very same that I see and love. Hence the disagreement between us seems to escape from the realm of literary criticism. We differ not about the nature of Milton's poetry, but about the nature of man, or even the nature of joy itself.[28]

The comparison with this disagreement is illuminating, for

the disagreement over Lawrence seems to be very like it— one whose source is a disagreement over 'the nature of man' and 'the nature of joy'. So the question of the validity of the critics' accounts is revealed to be essentially a moral one; it is our moral views which determine whether we react favourably or unfavourably to Lawrence, and therefore our moral views which ultimately determine our acceptance or rejection of a particular critical account of his work, and therefore the validity of that account. It is likely, then, that how we will react to Lawrence, and therefore how we react to these critics, will already have been decided to some extent before we ever reach the work or the critics. We have a prior view of how things are, and of how things ought to be, so that when we read the serious and insistent Lawrence we will already be predisposed either to like or dislike him. The analytic arguments of the critics will be secondary to these strong preconceptions, and it is unlikely that they will be powerful enough on their own to be able to change them, unless our moral views are already in a state of flux, and therefore open to influence. The work is also secondary to our preconceptions, though it is more possible that the work could exert enough power to change them. People do undergo changes in their moral views; and this perhaps explains why people are prone to dramatic changes of heart about Lawrence. The fact that people disagree in such an extreme way over Lawrence may also be due to the moral source of their response to him; people can differ strongly in their moral views, and they tend to feel more vehement about those views than about any others.

But that this disagreement over Lawrence is essentially a moral one does not put it outside our proper consideration. The accounts the critics give, though they may be determined by their moral feelings, are in terms of the text— this is where they locate their response; and whether we accept or reject a particular account depends on how we respond when we read the work. So it is how we respond to the work which is the immediate test of how we feel about Lawrence, and therefore of the validity of the critics' accounts, for, as we have shown, this is a case where validity depends on acceptance.

Nor is the nature of the disagreement simplified by our

seeing that its source is a moral one. For although two of the questions which the critics are answering when they pronounce judgement on Lawrence are moral — has Lawrence perceived a truth about human nature, and has he placed the right value on it? — the third is, as befits their role, a 'literary' one — has he given it true expression?

But can these moral questions really be separated from the final 'literary' one, or is this an artificial breakdown of the source of the critics' disagreement? It is possible to imagine that one writer could express a perception in such a way that, reading him, we could see it as a truth and be persuaded of its importance, when normally we would reject it because of our moral preconceptions, and when no other writer could persuade us that this was an important truth. But this still returns us to the question of values. For our view of the writings depends on our view of the value of what is expressed there. We can admire what we once disapproved of, if it has been expressed in such a way as to change our moral standpoint. But if we admire a man's writing intellectually, whilst still abhorring his way of looking at things, it will be our moral response that will modify our response to the writing, and not vice versa. In any case, this is to make an artificial distinction; for there can be an integral connection between what a man says and how he says it. It is no accident, for example, that Hitler's manner of expression strikes us as a physical manifestation of his views, and equally abhorrent. Thus, though it's possible to drive a wedge between the moral and the 'literary' questions, in the case of Lawrence it is not realistic to do so, for there is an inherent connection between his manner of expression and what he expresses.

The question now arises, is this really a case of critical disagreement, when it is a moral issue which is central? Moral questions, are, however, as much the domain of the critic as stylistic ones, so the fact that this is a disagreement over values does not preclude it from critical discussion. But what is more disturbing here is that the moral disagreement is disguised by the stylistic one. Leavis' arguments in *D.H. Lawrence: Novelist* are characteristically analytic, giving accounts of the power of the writing; and the doubts Huxley points to are expressed in the same terms. The reader or critic tends to locate his satisfaction or dissatisfaction in the manner of expression — structure, metaphor, use of languages, etc. — and ignores its deeper source, which is what is expressed. Leavis' moral stance is implicit in his arguments, it is true; but the centrality of his approval of Lawrence's perceptions should be more clearly recognised.

Where does this leave the critical arguments themselves, the analytic accounts of why Lawrence affects us as he does? Are they no more than rationalisations of the critics' response? They do spring from that response but at the same time they are articulations of how the critic feels about the actual writing. His location of his response in the writing itself may not go deep enough; but he is right in so far as the manner of expression is part of what is expressed. The arguments a critic uses to support his views can be very powerful and persuasive; Leavis' arguments, for instance, are characteristically intelligent and sensitive, well-supported from the text, and rhetorically powerful. We might even owe our appreciation of Lawrence to these arguments — Leavis may have opened up the work for us, and made us able to respond to Lawrence.[29] But this is no proof of the independent validity of such arguments. We may go through a stage, in cooling towards Lawrence, when Leavis' arguments still hold all their power for us, but when we are disappointed by the work itself. This is a tribute to the strength of Leavis' writings. But eventually, if the novel continues to give the lie to his critical accounts of them, his arguments will lose even their apparent cogency. They will begin to seem superficial, and finally, worthless; for their worth depends on their convincing us when we read the work.

2 The nature of critical arguments

Our central concern in the first chapter was to establish, not so much the diversity of critical judgements, for that is clear, but their great richness and complexity, which is often concealed by grammatical simplicity and sometimes by critical obviousness.

Now demonstrating that richness and complexity involved asking questions about what a judgement presupposed or implied, and about its correctness and how this would be shown. So, in our first chapter, we raised questions which are central to the second. One of these important and difficult questions is: when critics see their responses to works of literature as *correct*, how do they attempt their professional task of showing that the judgements in which those critical responses are articulated *are* correct? However, our concern is not merely anthropological, as it were. In discussing how critics proceed we shall also be raising the questions: are their procedures cogent? Do the arguments of critics demonstrate their claims? Could they do so?

Again, we proceed by examining a variety of cases. But we begin with a dual example of a form of critical argument which, we believe, is highly characteristic of criticism.

1. We shall examine part of an argument put forward by Leavis in his revaluation of Shelley, and an attack on it by R.H. Fogle.[1]

In what respects are the 'loose clouds' like 'decaying leaves'? The correspondence is certainly not in shape, colour, or way of moving. It is only the vague general sense of windy tumult that associates the clouds and the leaves[2]

To Mr. Leavis' objections to the comparison of 'loose clouds' with 'decaying leaves' *one can only assert* that there are quite adequate resemblances between them. The clouds and the leaves are carried in precisely the same fashion by the power of the wind. Furthermore, the resemblance holds for shape and colour as well as movement. Swift-flying clouds may present the same angularities as leaves, and leaves flying horizontally through a grey sky will take the hue of their surroundings.[3] (*Our italics*)

What is at issue here? Leavis thinks, not that Shelley's poetry or this poem is poor, rather that Shelley does have a genius, which this poem exemplifies, but that it is flawed and inferior, and Fogle disagrees. The quoted passages show that this disagreement is conducted in terms of the imagery; does the imagery, of which this image is representative, 'work'? Leavis says that it doesn't; in saying this he recognises that it may work for, and please, certain people, but his view is that it doesn't and shouldn't please anyone of true sensibility and judgement. In trying to give his reasons for his position Leavis talks about the 'vague general sense of windy tumult'; that 'vague' is pejorative, and Leavis tries to find some feature in the poem which both gives rise to and answers to this vagueness. (The relationship Leavis is looking for here is a causal one, but not just a causal one. It is not a relationship of the sort that exists between a man's failure in life and his consequent rise in blood pressure, but rather one of the sort which exists between a man's failure and his subsequent feelings of disappointment.) What he finds is what he calls 'a weak grasp upon the actual',[4] what elsewhere he might call lack of 'particularity';[5] and this in turn is constituted by and explained in terms of the lack of real similarities in the imagery, and specifically in this image the lack of real 'correspondence' between loose clouds and decaying leaves.

This then is Leavis' argument. But Fogle disagrees with what is apparently its conclusion; that is, he doesn't find the poem defective— that is *his* conclusion— and, accepting the terms in which Leavis conducts the argument, he does not find that this representative image fails to work. He therefore argues that the image does have particularity and seeks, as the quotation shows, to demonstrate that there are many resemblances between loose clouds and decaying leaves. He treats Leavis' 'argument' as an argument, and attempts to show that its 'premises' are false.

But what Fogle has to show is not merely that there are resemblances between clouds and leaves, but that these are 'adequate'. Now what would it be for these to be adequate? Do there have to be a lot of them?[6] Or do at least some of them have to be of a certain sort? If they do, of what sort should they be? How, in any case, does one list or count similarities? Is it not the case that we would see the resemblances between clouds and leaves as adequate if and when the image in which they were linked *worked* for us, i.e. when it struck us as apt, illuminating, powerful, etc?

It would seem that in these critical arguments it is the 'conclusion' which, as J.L. Austin would have said, 'wears the trousers'. That is, the conclusion is probably prior temporally, and is prior logically, to the particular observations the critic uses to support it. To say this is not to say that what Fogle mentions, and in particular his listing the similarities he sees between clouds and leaves, may not transform our view of the image; but it *need* not. And if it doesn't, we will say that the similarities are not of the right sort, or, with Leavis, that the image reveals 'a weak grasp on the actual'. This is one of various phrases he uses to try to locate and convey what it is in the poem that is lacking and which renders it defective.

Conversely, if, after reading Leavis, we still enjoy reading Shelley we will say that Leavis' particular observations are false, or that though they are not false, indeed they are extremely persuasive, he must have left something out of his account of the work; or that his view of that for which we may legitimately have an appetite is too narrow. It is our experience of the work, before or after having read what these critics have to say, which determines whether we accept their arguments, even though it may be the argument which helps to create that experience.

In this way the critical arguments under examination are quite unlike mathematical ones, where we do not begin with our answer to a problem and attempt to rationalise it; mathematical arguments indeed *demonstrate*, not merely in the literary critical sense of showing, but in the sense of proving, that our most certain intuitions can be quite wrong.[7] One can see now why such philosophers as F. Cioffi[8] and A. Isenberg[9] want to say that in critical arguments we begin with our conclusions.

To begin with one's conclusions may sound a question-begging, irrational way in which to conduct an argument. On the other hand, it may seem obvious that our experience of the poem, or whatever, must be that with which we begin the critical tasks of articulating that response and defending and explaining it. But the first thesis of this discussion is not trite if we distinguish the genetic banality from what, construed as a logical thesis, may be dubious. That is to say, *of course*, no doubt, the critic — the 'ideal reader' — begins the critical task with his reading of the poem. But it may still be true (in some cases it is true) that his reading, his experience of the work is, or ought to be, tested against the applicability of generally defined terms which serve the critic as his criteria of aesthetic worth. Even so, the irrationality of criticism, where it occurred, would not consist in a critic's beginning with his conclusions, however that phrase was to be construed in a particular case. We should rather speak of irrationality when a man insists on his view of a work and is, indeed, gripped by it, even when discussion reveals that he has not noticed important features in the work, when his response seems to be determined by, or is justified in terms of, factors which strike us as irrelevant, etc.

The proposed account of the nature of the disagreement between Leavis and Fogle does not mean, nor is it true, that they can only, simply and directly, contradict each other. There are various ways in which that disagreement might be pursued. Thus, a wedge might be driven between Leavis' particular observation and his overall view by challenging the background of assumptions against which the 'move' from one to the other is made, though the suggestion that there is indeed a move is misleading. Thus one might argue that the image Leavis singles out is not characteristic of Shelley's imagery, though this might itself involve establishing that not just one but a whole host of images had particularity. Or one could agree that the image is characteristic, yet find, and so argue, that it does have a certain precision, in that it exactly enacts the windiness of what it is describing. Or one might concede that the individual images lack precision but find that the whole poem has a feeling of 'windy tumult' which is exactly appropriate to the subject matter as a whole, and so *does* have a marvellously appropriate precision.[10] Or, as Fogle himself goes on to argue, one might say that particularity is not always a *desideratum* in poetry; if it were, poetry would be a lesser, narrower thing.

Such procedures as these could be appropriate and effective, and since, at least initially, they remove us from a situation in which the critics are simply contradicting each other, they may strike us as rational. But even if a man were forced to abandon any of these assumptions, his experience of the work might still compel him to say that the work was defective, and this need not be mere obduracy. And even if one could make progress through these different procedures, very often they involve settling matters of the same sort as those involved in the original disagreement, and it may still be the experience of the work which is the dominant factor. In any case, as these arguments become more abstract they take us away from the poetry and so run the risk of becoming unreal. A critic may not be guilty of intellectual myopia or provincialism if such abstract discussions make him feel that he wants to get back to his proper concern, the work itself.

   But since, apparently, our experience of the work can 'refute' either Fogle's or Leavis' argument— in so far as we can speak of 'refutation' here — should we categorise the series of remarks they make in expounding their positions *arguments* at all?[11]

   In fact, the dominance of the 'conclusion' is not peculiar to such arguments. It is a feature of any activity in which we are trying to describe, predict, explain, or justify events reported in statements the truth of which can be identified independently of others from which they may be deduced. For example, a patient may say apologetically, after receiving treatment that is invariably effective, 'But I'm afraid it still hurts'. Or an astronomical observer may say, 'Well, that planet isn't where it "ought" to be!' Such events refute the scientists' arguments, or at least force their modification, and can lead to a revision in their theories. We would think this feature demonstrated something very odd and suspect about the nature of many critical arguments only if we made the mistake of thinking that an observation could never overthrow an argument.

What distinguishes critical arguments from scientific ones, at least as some of the latter are presented by philosophers of science, is that the former are rarely presented in deductive form, though some at any rate could be. The reasons for this are complex but include the following: that deductive arguments which explain and justify their conclusions often include general or universal statements, and critics are usually very reluctant to commit themselves to substantive or normative generalisations, much less universal ones. (Leavis is most explicit about this.[12]) This is because they are aware that art objects, and our aesthetic, critical responses to them, are usually too complex and particular to make any but the roughest generalisations possible.[13] So a critical argument's being presented in a formally valid way can rarely strengthen it as an account of how we do, or should, see, or feel and think about, a work. If a reader who has accepted the premisses of such an argument finds the conclusion unconvincing when he returns to the work, he will experience little hesitation in deciding that something must be wrong with one or more of the assertions which led to it (cf. Fogle's ' . . . one can only assert . . .' *ibid.*) Stating an argument formally, which is in effect something R. Wellek once asked Leavis to do[14], but he declined,[15] might sometimes help to locate the theoretical or ideological differences between critics. But untheoretical, anti-ideological critics, if not others, are more likely to feel that the work itself is, of course, the source of a correct view and the critical task is to present this (cf. Leavis, below, pp. 54–5).[16] These demonstrations[17] are not proofs and, even in technical matters, i.e. where the critic is concerned to locate the source of a certain effect, are rarely much like experiments. They are more often characterizing[18], sensitising remarks, which 'give a face'[19] to the work, often including attempts to recreate the impression of the work itself.[20]

A sceptic who has accepted our account of arguments like Leavis' and Fogle's may still feel that these cannot be *real* arguments since they can be 'refuted' by anyone who (having read the poem and shown that he has some minimal understanding of it) disagrees with either conclusion. What he forgets, however, is that we often do broadly agree with judgements and arguments like Leavis'; there is an enormous amount of overlapping judgement concerning literature, and the other arts, which we tend to forget about, probably because these judgements are critical banalities. And if we did not sometimes agree, critical arguments would be otiose, given the then dubious assumption that we had an objective idiom in which to express them. In this respect criticism is not different from any other enquiry. Furthermore, the experience of having one's view of a work crystallised or even transfigured by reading a good critic like Leavis is not uncommon, and, again, if this were not so we should scarcely engage in this critical activity.

But this is not to suggest that Leavis' argument, however persuasive some of us may find it as a piece of criticism, is unproblematic, and we shall try to add to our understanding of it by next considering how Leavis' critical terms are defined and their correct application determined. He stresses that their meaning is bound to the context in which they are used; we can only fully understand what they mean when we see how they apply in specific cases:

I do not argue in general terms that there should be 'no emotion for its own sake, no afflatus, no mere generous emotionality, no luxury in pain and joy', but by choice arrangement and analysis of concrete examples I give those phrases (insofar, that is, as I have achieved my purpose) a precision of meaning they couldn't have got in any other way. There is, I hope, a chance that I may in this way have advanced theory even if I haven't done the theorising.[21]

Notice Leavis' first sentence here: 'I do not argue in *general* terms that there should be "no emotion for its own sake..."'. The suggestion is that, however, in each particular case he does argue precisely that; that in those cases which can be seen to exemplify any of the qualities he mentions here, it is these qualities which constitute the work's poorness. Similarly, in those places where the quality of particularity which Leavis admires can be seen, it is that particular particularity which constitutes the work's goodness! The connection between awareness of the trait and the evaluation is thus an immediate one and to *show* that a work has particularity is to show that and how it is good.

Now if the connection between the trait and the evaluation is immediate, the connection between the descriptive and the evaluative content of Leavis' critical terms must be an internal one. But this might elicit the objection from Fogle that although no doubt the descriptive and evaluative dimensions of the meaning of such a phrase as 'weak grasp on the actual' are internally related, Leavis can, and has, misapplied it, for he has failed to notice the real similarities between leaves and clouds. And both critics and philosophers will be exercised by how the correct application of such phrases is to be determined. (We return to this question.) A more radical objection to what is implicit in Leavis' position would come from those many distinguished philosophers — David Hume, G.E. Moore, A.J. Ayer, R.M. Hare — who believe that although words and phrases may have both descriptive and evaluative dimensions of meaning, their connection cannot be internal, i.e. logical, but must reflect the appetites and preferences of those who use them. So if the 'inference' from a work's exhibiting 'particularity' to its being good is immediate, and it appears to be so for Leavis, this is and must be because such terms lack determinate descriptive content. For although they cannot be used to pick out any quality in a work, what they are used to pick out is not determined by their descriptive meaning but depends on and reflects Leavis' preferences.[22] This is a major philosophical issue and we can only remark the existence of such words as 'true', 'valid', 'intelligent', and in certain uses perhaps, 'adult' and 'serious' where the connection does seem internal.

More frequently, however, Leavis seems to want to resist there being an immediate connection between a critical awareness of certain characteristics in a work and an evaluation. The former leads to the latter, not invariably perhaps, and certainly not immediately, but not contingently either. His arguments are more often conducted in this apparently Wittgensteinian way:

There is, then, an obvious sense in which Shelley's poetry offers feeling divorced from thought— offers it as something opposed to thought. *Along* with this characteristic goes Shelley's notable inability to grasp anything— to present any situation, any observed or imagined actuality, or any experience as an object existing independently in its own nature and in its own right. *Correlatively* there is the direct offer of emotion— emotion insistently explicit — in itself, for itself, for its own sake; we find our description merging into criticism . . . In the examination of his poetry the literary critic finds himself passing, by inevitable transitions, *from describing characteristics to making adverse judgements about* emotional quality; and so into a kind of discussion in which, by its proper method and in pursuit of its proper ends, literary criticism becomes the diagnosis of what, looking for an inclusive term, we can only call spiritual malady.[23] (Our italics)

However, it is fairly clear that the 'move' from 'describing' Shelley's poetry as offering 'feeling divorced from thought' to making an adverse judgement is, for Leavis anyway, not a move or an inference at all. Its offering feeling divorced from thought is a *part,* and a very important part, of the particular way in which Shelley's poetry is flawed. What are connected in a Wittgensteinian way are a series of 'characteristics' which are defects which together gravely reduce the merit of the poetry— and, perhaps, enable us to make adverse judgements about Shelley as author.

But *is* a 'weak grasp on the actual' a 'characteristic' of Shelley's poetry? As we know, informed readers disagree, and it would seem clear that in trying to answer this question there is no alternative to reading, or re-reading, the poem to see whether phrases such as 'weak grasp on the actual', 'a vague sense of windy tumult', 'feeling divorced from thought', etc., seem to characterise (any part of) our experience of the poem. Perhaps Fogle sees what Leavis sees but values it differently. And if that is not possible, who is to say which critic sees what is really there?

We have now reached a problem that is both critical and philosophical. Leavis' key critical terms and phrases are offered as indissolubly describing and evaluating the works he discusses. Moreover, he claims that they are defined, or subtly redefined, in each context in which they are used. So when someone 'disagrees' with Leavis, how can we tell whether this is genuine disagreement? For Leavis can simply reply that the rival critic has not understood what a term like, say, 'feeling divorced from thought' means, or alternatively, though it comes to the same for Leavis, that he has not seen that quality, which is there, in the work. For Leavis, to see the qualities in the work and to see the high or defective *quality* of the work is the same; and so he seems to rule out the possibility that two persons might see the same trait but value it differently. Indeed, because the terms are defined by their application and because they are *Leavis'* terms,[24] he even rules out the possibility that his own aesthetic 'vision' might be defective.[25]

Readers who 'disagree' with Leavis may see this view, that these terms can't be defined generally, as evidence that he is guilty of obfuscation. However, there are terms in criticism which though general in their meaning, for they apply to a whole class of things and not just one thing, nonetheless identify features in such a way that we can only learn to use them, and in that sense comes to understand them and know their meaning, by being shown examples, and with some critical terms only through some lengthy coaching (cf. 'balance' in pictures, 'class' in a discussion of batsmen). 'Particularity' etc., may be terms of this sort, so Leavis need not be guilty of obfuscation. Indeed those who share his position will feel that he has identified and demonstrated the virtues and vices of various works, and has done this through a sensitive understanding of the connections we have been considering, that he has in fact revealed these connections and thus *has* 'advanced theory'.

The fact remains, however, that there are people who at least imagine they disagree with Leavis. They may think he has seen what is not there, or failed to see what is there, or has valued it wrongly. Leavis may, of course, be right, but he has not succeeded in demonstrating that he is right to some of his readers, including Fogle. Yet, this is not to suggest that there might be a different or better way of demonstrating the truth of certain critical judgements than Leavis employs in pieces like ' "Thought" and Emotional Quality' and 'Reality and Sincerity'. Our philosophical view of what is going on here is connected to the side we take in the critical dispute, though the connection isn't simple. For we may be hostile to the obfuscation and authoritarianism that Leavis' technique allows — indeed invites— while being entirely persuaded by his view of Shelley and of the appropriateness of the manner of its demonstration.

We have been arguing in effect that in his criticism of 'Ode to the West Wind' Leavis does not use 'weak grasp on the actual' or other similar phrases as a criterion, or on the basis of the applicability of other generally defined terms which themselves function as criteria. That is to say, he does not approach the poem with a general definition of that damning phrase, or others, to see if it applies; or — and this comes to the same thing here— if we wanted to say he does do that, the question 'Does this phrase apply?' can only be settled by reading the poem. And a reading of the poem which seemed to suggest that it did (or did not) apply could not be proved to be wrong (or right) by such procedures as listing similarities between leaves and clouds or trying to show that these were somehow unreal, though such procedures can have an effect on how we see the work. (If anyone thinks differently he should look again at Leavis' criticism and ask himself why it is that some readers who have an appetite for particularity, etc., do not find it lacking in the poem.)

Leavis is making a similar point about criteria when he writes in a well-known metaphorical passage:

The critic— the reader of poetry— is indeed concerned with evaluation, but to figure him as measuring with a norm which he brings up to the object and applies from the outside is to misrepresent the process. . . . He doesn't ask 'How does this accord with these specifications of goodness in poetry?'; he aims to make fully conscious and articulate the immediate sense of value that 'places' the poem.[26]

A difficulty in giving an acceptable account of Leavis' procedure is that he also writes as if the flaws in Shelley's poem would be proved, indeed *have* been proved, by his analysis. And we do not want to suggest, nor does Leavis, that he does not have a set of values which could be elicited from this and other analyses.

We have drawn attention to certain similarities between Leavis' criticism of Shelley and the way in which we try to get others to see an aspect of something, say the man in the moon — or leaves like clouds. We have suggested that the disagreement between Fogle and Leavis resembles the disagreement between two persons who, for example, see a smile differently, one seeing it as threatening and the other as benevolent. Disagreements like this are not, or very rarely, settled by stricter definitions of 'threatening' or by finer measurements of the face. And what we say in getting someone to see the man in the moon is not a proof; we 'demonstrate', i.e. show, how the moon looks if and when we get others to see in it what we see.

But similes, or similarities, like these remind us that we cannot see anything as anything; there is right and wrong here, some smiles do not look threatening and cannot be seen as such. Similarly, we should have little difficulty in composing conventional, weak, clichéd verse which could not be seen as exhibiting particularity, and if we had greater difficulty in composing verse that demonstrated the virtue, that is mainly because it is difficult to write excellent verse.

That we do sometimes argue *to* an aesthetic appreciation of something, or prove that such a response is mistaken, is perhaps most clear when the response is to an object that is not a work of art. Some readers will have had the experience of being shown a very short proof in geometry (after having produced a very circuitous one themselves) and exclaiming

'Beautiful. How elegant!'. Of course, nothing can compel that aesthetic pleasure, though such a proof must command our purely mathematical approval. But the aesthetic response could not survive our discovering that the proof was invalid. Moreover, 'elegance' is specifiable fairly formally, partly and crucially in terms of length; and since shortness is economical and tends to reduce opportunities for mistakes, elegance — unlike particularity, perhaps — is scarcely a quality about whose desirability we might disagree. Similar remarks apply to what we feel and say about 'beautiful' experiments, and not too dissimilar ones about what we feel and say about the powers of observation and intelligence exhibited not only in non-literary writings but also in those offered as works of art. There is overlap here; which means that the account we have given of Leavis' criticism of Shelley and his disagreement with Fogle, will not fit all critical arguments.[27]

2. To illustrate how critical arguments may proceed from premises to conclusion, may indeed be logically demonstrative, we are going to examine some arguments taken from a critic whose work we examine a great deal in this book, Christopher Ricks. The arguments come from his defence of *Paradise Lost*. Our choice may seem paradoxical, even provocative, since, as Ricks himself points out, controversy over Milton started soon after the poem was published, and although his work has undoubtedly brought some changes in current views of Milton, disagreement persists. The explanation of this, insofar as a rational explanation is possible, is that Ricks' general position also depends on arguments which are not demonstrative, which indeed resemble Leavis' in the previous section, and which have not convinced all his readers.

Let us begin by quoting from three of the main participants in the dispute:

The Virgilian and Miltonic style is there to compensate for — to counteract — the privacy and informality of silent reading in a man's own study. Every judgement which does not realise this will be inept. To blame it for being ritualistic and incantatory, for lacking intimacy or the speaking voice, is to blame it for being just what it intends to be ... (Milton) therefore compensates for the complexity of his syntax by the simplicity of the broad imaginative effects beneath it, and the perfect rightness of their sequence. For us readers, this means in fact that our receptivity can be mainly laid open to the underlying simplicity, while we have only to play at the complex syntax. It is not in the least necessary to go to the bottom of these verse sentences as you go to the bottom of Hooker's sentences in prose.

C.S. Lewis, *Preface to Paradise Lost*
(Oxford, 1942), pp. 40, 45.

He has his 'music'. In this 'music', of course, the rhythm plays an essential part — the Grand Style movement that, compelling with its incantatory and ritualistic habit a marked bodily response, both compensates for the lack in the verse of any concrete body such as is given by stength of imagery, and lulls the mind out of its normal attentiveness. It is the lack of body — 'body' as I have illustrated it from Keats — that together with the lack in the sense of any challenges to a sharp awareness, makes us talk of 'music'

F.R. Leavis, *The Common Pursuit*
(London, 1952), pp. 17–18

They believe . . . that it *is* sensitive and subtle. That Milton *does* make use of expressive closeness to the senses when occasion demands. That his words are not sealed off as if they were in cellophane bags. And that our standards of relevancy and consistency must be as sharp as usual. My own preference is for this position.

Christopher Ricks, *Milton's Grand Style*
(Oxford, 1963) p. 9.

In the first argument we are concerned with Ricks is simply correcting a misreading. The lines in question are:

then let those
Contrive who need, or when they need, not now,
For while they sit contriving, shall the rest
Millions that stand in arms, and longing wait
The signal to ascend, sit ling'ring here
Heav'ns fugitives . . .

Paradise Lost, (11.52–7)

These have been chronically misread as containing a contrad-iction between 'stand' and 'sit ling'ring', and Lewis has used this example to support his view that the music of Milton's rhetoric disguises its lack of 'concrete body'. Here is Ricks' reply:

> But is it possible to accept the demand for consistency and still defend Milton here? Of course.
>
> Mr. Eliot's slip (and Dr. Leavis') is in objecting that 'Millions that stand in arms could not at the same time sit lingering'. They could not, but Milton doesn't say they could. He has a future and a present tense:
>
> > *Shall* the rest,
> > Millions that stand in arms, and longing wait
> > The signal to ascend, sit ling'ring here . . .
>
> There is no inconsistency here . . . .
>
>

Milton's Grand Style pp. 11–12

Ricks is unproblematically right here; the lines do contain a future tense, which others have failed to notice, and so are not contradictory. The claim is a logical one and has that sort of status and certainty.

Of course, this is a very small point, but necessary for Ricks to go on to argue a larger one; demonstrating that many critics have misread at this level paves the way for demonstrating that they have failed to appreciate the subtleties of the passage and their point. Ricks' second argument runs thus:

> (Moloch) brilliantly numbers those that are of his way of thinking (and acting), and contrasts their military stance with the sitting about of the not-numbered 'they':
>
> > shall the rest
> > Millions that stand in arms, and longing wait
> > The signal to ascend . . .
>
> And at that dramatic point, the superb upward thrust of 'sit', 'stand', 'ascend', is razed by the deliberate bathos of 'sit' again:
>
> > Millions that stand in arms, and longing wait
> > The signal to ascend, sit ling'ring here . . .

The contrivers (the Belials) want to turn standers into sitters. And with fighting skill, Moloch answers the participle 'sit contriving' with the same construction in 'sit ling'ring'. Men who stand will be made to sit.

Ibid., pp. 12–13

Ricks here shows that the passage is not gratuitously complex. The separation of 'shall' from 'sit ling'ring' (which is probably responsible for the common misreading), the repetition of 'sit' with a present participle, the clash of 'sit' and 'stand', even the meandering construction — which Ricks suggest parodies the long-winded speech of the 'contrivers' — , these devices, which involve sound, sense and syntax, have dramatic, rhetorical and so poetic point and function. Ricks shows that these lines do provide a challenge to the reader's 'sharp awareness', that if we do not 'go to the bottom' of them, if we 'play at' their syntax their meaningful complexity will be lost in the mere 'music' of the lines.

Here then we have arguments in support of the two claims, that the lines make literal sense, and that their complexity is not gratuitous. The premisses of these arguments are the lines themselves. Ricks' analysis of them does not add to the evidence they provide, it makes it evident. Thus any criticism of these lines which involves denying either thesis is mistaken in *its rationale*.

But to put the point carefully in this way is to raise the question, is Ricks' analysis of such a sort that we cannot properly disagree with his evaluation of the lines? Couldn't a critic hostile to Milton concede all that Ricks has proved, but still maintain that the lines don't *work*?

Our answers here must be yes, for two reasons. Ricks' analysis, detailed though it is, is not exhaustive, and other features in the passage could both explain and warrant a negative response. We can best illustrate this by referring to another passage in which Ricks defends Milton's lines.

> 'Aire, Water, Earth,
> By Fowl, Fish, Beast, was flown, was swum, was walkt
> Frequent'
>
> (vii 502–4)

Ricks show that this construction, which may have struck us as latinate and artificial is not just that, the passive construction indicates the subjugation of the grammatical subject (and hence here suggests the subjugation of the elements to God). He does however concede that this is not Milton at his best; and it may be that here our appreciation of the conceptual point made by the passive construction is modified by its artificiality in relation to verbs which are usually in the active voice.

In any case, suppose that Ricks' analysis were more exhaustive than it is. (The notion of a 'complete' analysis is not clear, but it is clear that a highly detailed critical analysis would mention not only the meanings of words and the grammatical construction of lines — and in so doing demonstrate perhaps they they do make sense — but the connotations of words, their sounds — alliteration, assonance, etc. — rhythm, emphasis, and so on.) Would adding to Ricks' analysis of Moloch's lines overcome the objections of those who find the lines awkward and disagreeably latinate? (We scarcely need to hypothesise readers of such a sort.) And if it did not do so, what *proof* would the more complete analysis be that a reader should not feel like this about the lines? He is not guilty of conceptual error and (if only after having read Ricks) he has not failed to notice the construction of the lines, etc. So the charge would be that he is insensitive to the qualities of the complex latinate construction— perhaps because of his lack of acquaintance with Latin and Latin verse. But ignorance is not insensitivity; and if a grounding in Latin verse does in fact turn out to be necessary for an appreciation of Milton's poetry, is this not a criticism? This question cannot be answered by an analysis of Milton's lines, and is clearly of a sort and scale that is not amenable to proof.

Now Ricks himself is well aware of the limitations of criticism in *proving* the existence of a feature in the poem:

Plainly there is no theory or dial which will tell whether or not a particular critical insight is true. We cannot expect *proof*; but we have a right to some degree of substantiation— an insight must be plausible. Naturally there are moments when critics may seem to be proclaiming 'the more the merrier' — the more suggestions, or ambiguities, or paradoxes, the better the poem. But one's objections may not be to their creed, but to the particular moments when their creed does not fit the evidence, when it demands that we reject the different kinds of substantiation to which one may appeal: the aptness of the insight itself, both locally and in the poem as a whole; the practice of the poet elsewhere; the practice of his contemporaries; the observations of his critics, especially the earliest ones; and so on. In each case there will be a unique balance of evidence.

Milton's Grand Style pp. 20–1

Yet even where we can establish the existence of certain features in a poem, this, as we've been arguing, doesn't in all cases establish how we should respond to them, so that what critical analysis can establish is still further limited. Even with regard to what we have been calling conceptual matters a gap can appear between demonstrating that a poem, say, makes literal sense and proving that it should do so when we read it. Precisely this gap seems to open up in the case of *Paradise Lost*. For many skilled and sympathetic readers the poem is so dense and difficult — and *long* — that they cannot sustain a reading that goes to the bottom of every sentence. Lewis himself may be such a reader and perhaps that is why he thinks that his is the appropriate reading. A poem is not a mathematical treatise, and if it is difficult to follow it may be deficient as well as the reader.

Having said this, we would insist that Ricks' reading is the fuller one which makes the best poem, so long as it can be sustained over short passages; and it is difficult to believe that even those who read — or think they read — Milton for his music can read him in very long stretches. What Ricks' whole analysis, of which what we have called the second argument is a very small part, can do is draw our attention to features in the poetry which at some level we may have seen but not recognised; by so doing it may not only change our belief about the construction of the poetry but transform our experience of the poem.

So the critic may correct our misreadings, draw our attention to features in works which we had not noticed, recharacterise features which we had noticed, etc., and in so doing change our beliefs about, experience, and valuing, of a work. Deductive arguments may sometimes have a role to play, including those with purely conceptual premises (as we have just shown), but a critic's 'argument', i.e. what he has to say, will much more frequently, and characteristically, contain remarks whose test will be his reader's experience of the work after he has read the criticism (cf. our discussion of Leavis).

The collection of logically disparate remarks which usually make up a piece of criticism also contains some which have, or appear to have, a causal dimension (not necessarily excluding those mentioned in the last paragraph). Thus, the critic may mention e.g., rhyme or rhythm and say that it has a certain effect. Of course these remarks often have a predictive dimension. This feature will have that effect, when you notice it; which removes the paradox that the critic appears sometimes to be explaining the genesis of effects not felt by some of his readers. They also characteristically carry a normative dimension too. This feature should have that effect, i.e., it will, and does, on persons of proper sensibility, but, as we argue later, this dimension does not preclude the causal one, as some philosophers of criticism have thought, but requires it. Still, that critics *do* engage in making causal judgements does seem to raise a problem, for it would seem that a rigorous examination of them should require the reader to perform experiments, and this surely is something we do not do either in reading, or writing, criticism?

We are now raising questions that we shall pursue throughout the rest of this book. But in the remainder of this chapter, we shall be examining, by challenging, critical arguments which, or in so far as they, attempt to explain how poems, or parts of poems, 'work'. In so doing we shall show that these claims are sometimes not factual or, more specifically, causal, despite superficial appearances to the contrary, and, conversely, that they sometimes are causal and yet are not always, therefore, decidable even by means of experiment.

3.　　　　　　　　Fall, winter, fall; for he
　　　　　　　　　Prompt hand and headpiece clever,

Has woven a winter robe,
And made of earth and sea
His overcoat forever,
And wears the turning globe.

Housman has been very daring here. The metaphor with which the poem ends is as bizarre and witty as one of John Donne's. For the speaker insists that the earth has not swallowed up Dick but that the dead man has wrapped the earth about himself 'and wears the turning globe'. For a poet so Victorian in his tastes as Housman was, a poet generally so inimical to witty conceits, his conceit of Dick's wearing the globe is very curious indeed. But the bold figure works. The suggestion of schoolboy slang, 'prompt hand and head-piece clever', helps to prepare for it, and something of extravagance is needed if the poem is not to dissolve into a kind of too pure and direct pathos. But what makes the last lines work is Housman's audacity in using the commonplace and matter-of-fact word 'overcoat'. He has already called it a 'winter robe' and now if he were to name it a 'cloak' or a 'toga' or even a 'garment' the poem would close on a kind of strained embarrassment. But 'overcoat' here is triumphantly right. It represents the brilliant handling of tone which is to be found in nearly all of Housman's successful poems.
Cleanth Brooks, *A Shaping Joy: Studies in the writer's craft* (London, 1971), p. 298.

Perhaps precisely because Brooks' view of the poem may not persuade us, we may be impressed by the apparent paucity of his arguments concerning how it works. For instance, he says that the second line carries a suggestion of schoolboy slang, but gives no evidence for what is apparently a claim of substance. Then he moves from this unsupported claim to a further one, namely that this tone helps to prepare us for the bizarre nature of the final conceit. And he suggests that 'overcoat' works by introducing an unexpected down-to-earth tone, coming where a word like 'toga' might have been more consistent with the overall style of the poem. In fact, his argument consists of a series of assertions.

But its apparent lack of rigour may, at least in places, come to no more that this — that it fails to persuade. At these points if it persuades, what more should we ask? And if it fails to persuade, what more might tip the scales? The reply would seem to be, further argument. But of what sort would this be? It could only be interpolations of a logically similar sort to those Brooks already gives us, which would consist in saying such things as 'Is not this apt?', 'Is not that unhappy?', 'Can't you see that this is inappropriate because of that?'. And in all these cases, the correctness of what is asserted comes to no more than our seeing the assertion as correct.

'But surely', it might be objected, 'it is a *fact* as to whether or not "headpiece" is, or was, schoolboy slang?' However, whether it is, or was, schoolboy slang is not to the point, and, unusually, the actual wording of the critic's remark in this case does not belie our claim but confirms it. For what Brooks says is that the line in which 'headpiece' occurs *suggests* schoolboy slang, and its doing so does not depend on whether 'headpiece' is indeed schoolboy slang. Not everything that is schoolboy slang will sound as if it is, and vice versa.

The preceding points might be conceded, but it still might be asserted that whether a word 'suggests schoolboy slang' is every bit as much a fact as whether it is schoolboy slang. That is to say, the truth of what Brooks claims does not depend, as we allege, on our accepting it as correct.

Now, there are contexts in which an experimental construction of 'suggests' would be appropriate, that is, contexts in which we would determine whether or not A suggests B by asking subjects, 'What does A suggest?'. But there are other contexts, and we claim that this is one, in which 'testing' would be of a different sort. We ask the subject the loaded question, 'Doesn't A suggest B?' and if he says that it does, it does. In this context whether A suggests B depends on whether readers accept that the second line of the stanza suggests schoolboy slang— which is the sort of construction we put on Brooks' phrase, and certain of his others.

But what proof is there that we have put the right, or appropriate, construction on Brooks' claim? There is no *proof*. Ours is an empirical thesis about how in fact remarks of this sort are treated by critics and readers of criticism. Readers of criticism might test Brooks' claim in an experimental manner, but — and it is otiose to say this — they do not do so. Moreover, if a reader were to proceed in this fashion we suspect that he would be regarded as philistine or silly— at any rate, as not having learnt how criticism proceeds.

It may occur to our readers that Brooks' claim, though correctly characterised as non-substantial, may get transformed into a substantial claim and a true one simply through its being read and accepted. For once this has happened, 'headpiece clever' will indeed suggest, in the empirical sense, schoolboy slang. In this way the appeal of a critical claim may be sufficient to transform it into a substantial truth.

4.
> So glistered the dire snake, and into fraud
> Led Eve, our credulous Mother, to the tree
> Of prohibition, root of all our woe.
>
> (*Paradise Lost*, IX 635–5)

These lines stamp themselves at once as in the Grand Style. What is remarkable, though, is that they are verbally subtle and active without any fussiness or any blurring of the grand austerity. I am thinking not only of the sombre gleam in the pun on 'root', but also of subtler effects: the playing of the bright 'glistered' against the dark 'dire', for instance. Or the superb use of the curt 'snake' . . . There is the superbly suggestive diction: 'our credulous Mother', which must be one of the finest, most delicate, and most moving of all the oxymorons in the poem. A mother ought to be everything that is reliable and wise — here she is credulous. And 'our' clinches the effect; 'credulous' is pinioned on each side ('our . . . Mother'), and the full tragic pathos of the oxymoron is released.

Christopher Ricks, *Milton's Grand Style* pp. 75–6

Ricks draws our attention to something that may easily be missed by the inattentive reader, *viz*., the fine, delicate, and moving quality of the phrase 'our credulous Mother' and he shows in a strikingly similar piece of criticism on the same passage[28] that this quality is lost if 'foolish' or 'gullible' are substituted for 'credulous'. It should be noticed here that if, after consideration, someone disagrees with this claim, the argument cannot proceed for him.

How then does the phrase work? Ricks says that a 'mother should be everything that is reliable and wise', presumably because either mothers are reliable and wise or because we expect them to be, so that the word 'mother' has this connotation. Thus 'credulous mother' will strike us as a conjunction of antitheticals; it will be oxymoronic. But is it? Does it strike us in this way? Since the claim is not about the definitions of these words but about their connotations, there can be no evidence on this matter beyond our reactions, either to the phrase itself, or to Ricks' claim about it, and once we have heard the claim we have lost our innocence over this issue. But, despite Ricks' claim, the phrase does not strike us as 'a brief paradox' (*ibid.*). In any case, if he were right here, then 'our gullible mother' and 'our foolish mother' would also be oxymoronic, yet, as he says, they lack the subtle power of Milton's chosen phrase.

Why is this? Ricks' explanation may be wrong, but we can only hazard guesses at a true explanation. However, it does seem that, for whatever reason 'credulous', unlike 'foolish' and 'gullible', is not always used in a condemnatory way. In attempting to explain this it might be said that a person cannot be condemned as credulous unless we can condemn him for his simplicity of mind or his lack of experience. But we cannot condemn anyone for being simple minded, and innocence itself, when being described in that way, strikes most of us who have been brought up in a Christian tradition as an excellent state. 'Credulousness' indicates a tender fault, where it is a fault at all. Its antitheses are 'suspiciousness', 'knowingness' and 'cynicism'. Unlike an individual's dishonesty, it could not be a fault in a world that was otherwise perfect.

Now Eve had already been warned at this point in the poem, she should not have believed the snake, but her doing so is described in a word that tenderly mitigates her error. A tension, then, lies within the word 'credulous', and the gentle, non-condemnatory connotations of the word are reinforced by calling Eve, as yet no-one's mother, 'our . . . Mother'. But this is not because a mother ought to be everything that is reliable and wise — that, indeed, should strengthen the condemnatory force of 'credulous' which may explain why 'our credulous Father' seems so belittling — but because mothers are softly and tenderly loving and loved; hence the reinforcing forces of 'our'. 'Our credulous Mother' then is not an oxymoron, the connotations of 'credulous' and 'mother' do not really clash and, if they did clash in the way in which Ricks claims they do, the phrase would be a harsh one, as, we have noted, is 'our credulous Father'. It is rather that the connotations of 'mother' reinforce the gentler aspects of, and our gentler feelings towards, being credulous.

The preceding argument shows that Ricks' argument is incomplete, at best, and explains nothing. Yet the attentive reader will realise that our explanation is, at best, incomplete. For virtually everything we said about 'credulous' might equally be said about 'gullible' and 'foolish', so our account, like Ricks', does not explain why 'our foolish Mother' or 'our gullible Mother' are not equally fine, subtle, and moving.

Perhaps it is simply a brute fact, depending on accidents of usage that, despite 'gullible' and 'foolish' having meanings which would permit them to be used non-condemnatorily, they, unlike 'credulous', are invariably used to condemn, so that they have pejorative connotations in a way and to a degree that 'credulous' does not; though whether this was true when Milton wrote *Paradise Lost* is another matter. Ricks, sensitive to the delicate power of the phrase, and its superiority over its variations, strives to explain it. And we readers, whose response to the phrase is confirmed, heightened, or even created by Ricks, may all too easily accept his explanation of it.[29]

Perhaps it should be said that we are not making the completely general point here that people are eager to accept explanations in whatever field they occur; though there may be some truth in this cynical claim. We are suggesting that this is true of literary criticism. Explanations, particularly those that appear to be relevant and which show an awareness of the complexity of a problem, are not always so common that we have to choose between them. In any case, little turns on acceptance or choice, as it does, say, in medicine, especially if explanations of this sort are characteristically inconclusive. We can thus enjoy the intellectual pleasure of being satisfied, without running the risk of being proved wrong or foolish. Because of this inconclusiveness we may also see competing explanations as indicating, not the chaotic state of criticism, but its richness.

Achieving a right view of Ricks' explanations of how the poetry works is further complicated by a fact mentioned earlier, *viz.*, that in reading this account we may not have discovered the explanation of a response we have already felt but we may have discovered the response itself. This is the more likely because Ricks combines his analytic account of an effect with an attempt to recreate or echo the effect. When he talks about the pun on 'root', for example, he does not explain its significance but instead attempts to convey the contrast it embodies, between levity and high seriousness, in the words 'sombre gleam'. One consequence of this manner of combining the revelation of how the effect is achieved with the revelation of the effect itself is that there exists an intimate connection in our minds between our response and the particular explanation of it.

Does this mean our response stands or falls with this particular explanation? No, the connection is not so direct, though if we were shown conclusively that Ricks' account of this passage were incorrect, we might not be able to maintain the same *particular* response to it; but our overall sense of its subtlety and effectiveness need not be affected. We could look around for other explanations of our response — though we might feel a certain unease about having a quite different explanation for our response than the one which actually led to it in the first place. And even if Ricks can be shown to be wrong, his criticism is worthwhile if he has made the work appreciable for us. It is not always necessary for the critic to perform this task, but where it is necessary no other task could be more important.

5.
>I made my song a coat
>Covered with embroideries
>Out of old mythologies
>From heel to throat.

In the slightly facile rhyme, 'embroideries/mythologies' one seems to detect a note of impatience with the muffling coat he is casting off, and a sense of sharpened anticipation is introduced by the feminine half-rhyme in the last three lines:

>Song let them take it
>For there's more enterprise
>In walking naked.

This eight-line poem, I suggest, contains not only Yeats' old style and his new, but inseparable from these, his early backward vision and his late prophetic vision.

J. Stallworthy, *Vision and Revision in Yeats' Last Poems*
(Oxford, 1969), p. 33).

It is rather puzzling that Stallworthy should quote seven lines of what he states is an eight-line poem. Moreover, in the complete poem there are in fact ten lines, and what is missing 'But the fools caught it, Wore it in the world's eyes As though they'd wrought it' (lines 5–7), suggests that Yeats was unhappy, not so much with the style of his earlier verse, but with the way in which the verse had been treated by others. Stallworthy's reading, therefore, seems somewhat distorted almost certainly by information that derives from beyond the text. In spite of this distortion, the first two claims he makes are characteristic of the claims critics make, they clearly make sense and are plausible and attractive. But are they true? And here what is in question is not so much the correctness of Stallworthy's interpretation but rather the correctness of his location of which part of the poem conveys the alleged 'impatience', and how it does this.

The first claim, a guarded and weak one, is that the 'slightly facile rhyme', of the second and third lines contains, expresses, or indicates Yeats' impatience with his earlier style, the earlier style which Stallworthy feels is echoed in the first four lines. If the rhyme does have this effect on sensitive readers of the poem, and it may do so without Yeats' either having felt this impatience or his having wished to indicate that he felt it, how does it do it? Stallworthy doesn't tell us, so we must reconstruct his argument.

The argument might run in various ways. We could see the rhyme as a facile one because it is a half-rhyme, and this might indicate that Yeats was impatient with his subject here, his old style, and did not want to waste time in thinking of a full rhyme. However, it might be said that it would be extremely difficult to find a full rhyme for 'embroideries', and so Yeats' not doing so would not warrant our seeing the half-rhyme as a sign of impatience. Nonetheless, it might give that impression unwarrantedly, and Yeats may have felt this himself, or used his intuitive knowledge of the way our minds work in order to get this effect, when constructing the verse.

A richer version of the argument could be that the facile nature of the rhyme, which is a point of stress in the poem, lies in the actual vocabulary Yeats has used here. In using 'embroideries' and 'mythologies', he has fallen back into the ornate, resonant, poetic diction of his earlier style. It might be argued that he has done this because he does not want to expend effort seeking out tauter, more economic vocabulary, as would be appropriate to his new style, because he is already impatient with and contemptuous of his subject. The resulting lack of effort reflected in the choice of words for the rhyme, and in the lazy half-rhyme shows Yeats' impatience. Stallworthy might be a little embarrassed by the arguments based on the facility of a half-rhyme, for in his second claim he sees a half-rhyme as showing something rather different. Here, his view is that the feminine half-rhyme, 'take it' and 'naked', in the last three lines of the poem, introduces a 'sense of sharpened anticipation'.

Again, we must hypothesise as to how Stallworthy would support this view, but he could do this. He might say that it is the combination of the half-rhyme with the final weak syllable which produces a sense of something unfinished and which leaves us hanging, in expectation, at the end of the poem. It produces, not just a sense that Yeats himself is uncertain, still developing the promise of his new style, in antithesis to his decisive dismissal of the old, but also a sense of anticipation in the reader, and expectation of what is to develop from that promise.

Why then should Stallworthy be embarrassed by the claim that the same device achieves different results in the poem? This is possible provided there are other variables to explain the differing effects. And there are — differing senses, the fact that 'take it/naked' is a *feminine* half-ryhme, the use of 'new' as opposed to 'old' vocabulary, and so on.

However, all we have established so far is that the explanations Stallworthy might give of how different effects are achieved by similar devices, half-rhymes, could be correct. But are they? These explanations appear to make sense, and they appeal to us. But this is insufficient for their being correct. In 1947, women's fashions were militaristic; the explanation that this was a result of the influence of the war seems highly plausible. But suppose the fashion had been extremely feminine; would not the same explanation seem equally plausible? We might complicate our explanations to make them look like explanations, and to avoid this sort of objection, but would our doing this show that the war was a factor at all?

In the case of Stallworthy's first claim, whatever explanation he might produce, at least he seems committed to this, *viz*., that a rhyme that was facile, and which also involved the old vocabulary, would produce this effect in these four lines. But at once we must enter a caveat and make a qualification. For it is clear that Stallworthy is committed to rather less than this, as some such rhymes would be so inappropriate, the meaning of the rhyming words would be so at odds with the rest of the verse, that they would destroy the sense of the whole. The substituted words must be appropriate. Stallworthy, then, is committed to the claim that, in this context, a facile rhyme using appropriate words drawn from the old vocabulary is sufficient to indicate a note of impatience. However, he is also committed to the claim that, in this context, the facile rhyme using old vocabulary is necessary for this effect, not in the sense that nothing else in this context could produce that effect, but that the note of impatience isn't produced solely by the other elements in the first four lines.

An analogy may help to illuminate the structure of this argument. In a given situation, a scientist might claim that an explosion resulted from the presence of gas in a piece of apparatus, its reaching a certain concentration, and then being ignited by a spark. If we produced the same concentration of gas in the apparatus and then a similar spark, and no explosion resulted, we could claim that, given that concentration of gas in the apparatus, it could not simply have been that spark which caused the explosion. That effect must depend on other factors which had not been isolated or mentioned in the scientist's account. Conversely, we could test his claim by showing that the spark was not necessary. But we could not do this by substituting another factor for the spark, for example, by heating the gas mixture. We must keep all other conditions the same, and not produce the spark. If the explosion still occurs, the spark is not necessary, and is not the cause, or even a cause, of the explosion.

Using this analogy as a guide, there are apparently two ways we could test Stallworthy's claims. Firstly, we could produce another pair of appropriate facilely rhyming words in Yeats' old style, and if the four lines did not then indicate Yeats' impatience with that old style, we would seem to have shown that Stallworthy's explanation of how this effect was achieved is incorrect. The result of this experiment would also seem to show that Yeats' rhyme was indeed doing the work, but in virtue of some characteristics other than its being facile.

But such an experiment would be difficult to perform, for it would be difficult— perhaps impossible— to find another pair of appropriate, facilely rhyming words in Yeats' old vocabulary. And even if we could perform the experiment, though it would be convincing, it would not be conclusive. For Stallworthy could coherently claim that it was precisely the *other* characteristics of the substituted rhyming words which prevented the facility of their rhyme and their being in the old vocabulary, from having its effect.

The critical experiment then is not quite like the scientific one. It is much more difficult to perform, and less conclusive, which may help to explain why such experiments are rarely attempted. In particular, we cannot produce anything precisely analogous to 'the same spark' without producing Yeats' rhyme itself. If we look for relevantly similar rhymes we may well lack the invention to find them, or they may simply not exist to be found. There are no difficulties of this sort in conducting the scientific experiment. There it is a matter of determining the characteristics of the original spark and making sure that these are retained in the experiment. Moreover, if we find an apparently similar pair of words to substitute for the originals, Stallworthy may claim that it is the ways in which they differ from those originals which prevents the ways in which they resemble Yeats' rhyming pair from having their effect. Stallworthy could be wrong here, but he could just be right. Or must we abandon the hope that this is an issue on which the critic could be shown to be right or wrong?

The other way we can try to test Stallworthy's claim that it is the facile half-rhyme, etc. which suggests Yeats' impatience, is to see if this effect is produced in the absence of the claimed cause. So we must remove Yeats' rhyme and be careful not to substitute anything else that might produce the effect. In the case of the scientific experiment this can be done easily enough, we just don't produce a spark. But if we attempt the analogue of this with poetry we get

> I made my song a coat
> Covered with
> Out of old
> From heel to throat

This certainly does not get the effect which Stallworthy finds in the original and which he attributes to Yeats' missing rhyme. But the 'experiment' in no way confirms his thesis. For when the rhyme is removed we are left with nonsense. The gaps are not, as it were, *nothing* and they produce effects of bewilderment, a feeling that something is missing or something has gone wrong, which swamp anything else we might feel about what we have before us.

There is, then, nothing we can do that is analogous to not reproducing a spark in the scientific experiment. All that we may deduce from our attempt at an analogous experiment with the verse is a platitude, *viz.*, that in the example a pair of words is necessary if the verse is to make any sense, and so *a fortiori* they are necessary for it to indicate Yeats' impatience with his old verse. But which words would do this, and how they would do it, remains as open a question as it was before we attempted our experiment. It is, then, quite pointless and again quite unlike the superficially analogous scientific experiment. No wonder it is not performed.

Are we not at an *impasse*? We are not unless it is sheer intellectual vulgarity which leads us to think that if the effect which Stallworthy claims is produced by the first four lines, were produced even if these four lines did not contain a 'slightly facile rhyme' in the old vocabulary, we would have refuted Stallworthy's explanation of how that alleged effect is produced. But perhaps it is not sheer intellectual vulgarity. To show that it is not, we must return to our scientific example. How does a scientist decide whether all the factors in an experiment are the same as in a previously performed experiment, or differ in one respect only? Doesn't a control experiment, for example, differ from the experiment for which it is a control by taking place on a different part of his bench, or on a different day? Why does he not mention the presence or absence of litmus paper on the laboratory bench in describing the boundary conditions in which the explosions occur or fail to occur?

The only answer there can be to this question is that features in a situation are treated as factors which contribute to what happens in that situation, if there is reason for thinking that they play a role in what happens. We believe that they play a role if we believe that these features are connected, and so, at least, correlated with what happens, and the basis for that belief, unless it is irrational, is that we have noticed such connections, or the connections can be seen to exist *a priori*.

So our question now is, have we noticed that facile rhymes in Yeats' old vocabulary tend to produce — and so, at least, tend to be associated with — impatience; and that rhymes of other sorts are not? It is only if we have noticed or have some other reason for believing this that our substituting a rhyme of another sort for Yeats' rhyme can be a test of Stallworthy's explanation. And it should be noticed here that in order to test Stallworthy's particular claim, it is necessary that the more general claim to which he is committed should be correct, i.e. that facile rhymes in Yeats' old vocabulary tend to produce this effect, and other rhymes do not. It is necessary that these claims should be true in order to determine whether Stallworthy's particular claim is true or false.

Are the general claims, then, true? One difficulty with this question is that one of the general claims — that facile rhymes in Yeats' old vocabulary are generally connected with our finding a note of impatience in the verses in which they occur — is scarcely general enough. Brushing aside this difficulty, let us ask instead, are not facile rhymes connected with, and so indicative of, impatience in authors? Interestingly, the answer to this question must be a qualified Yes, for we can 'see' how a man who is impatient while writing poetry might produce facile rhymes rather than non-facile ones, simply because the former are easier to find. But noticing the correlation between being impatient and producing facile rhymes is scarcely the basis for the belief that they are connected. It is rather the case that we see how one is the natural product or expression of the other. The belief that impatience is a state which is likely to produce things of this sort is, in that sense, an *a priori* one.

So a general claim, the truth of which is a prerequisite for the truth of Stallworthy's explanation, is true. We can now ask, is Stallworthy's explanation correct; and we can show it to be correct or incorrect by substituting a rhyme which is not facile and producing or not producing the effect— given the truth of the other general claim, namely that rhymes of this other sort are not connected with impatience.

Have we now cornered Stallworthy's argument? Unhappily, the answer must again be No, because although we have not noticed, and cannot see a connection between, non-facile rhymes and impatience, this is only because such rhymes don't form a true class. Within this heterogeneous collection, there may well be classes or sorts of rhymes which are connected with impatience. Moreover, a particular member of a true class of rhymes the members of which are not generally connected with, and so indicative of, impatience in their author, might nonetheless indicate impatience, because of their other features, the senses of the words rhymed, their associations for that author, and so on.

Our conclusion is, then, that an experimental testing of what indicates the alleged feeling of impatience which Stallworthy finds in the poem, and of how it does so, cannot succeed. We may lack the invention to find alternative words, or the words may not exist to be found, or, even if we succeed in finding some such words, they unavoidably must differ from Yeats' own words in more ways than their not being facile; and these differentiae may produce the effect which Stallworthy claims is produced by the facility of Yeats' rhymes, or alternatively they may inhibit the effect which their facility would produce, and which the facility of Yeats' rhyme does produce. Stallworthy may be right, he may bs wrong, but even if we treat his claims as quasi-scientific ones, i.e. as being inherently, though implicitly, general, they cannot be tested.

But what sort of impossibility are we confronted with here? It is a contingent matter that we lack invention, and a contingent matter that the words necessary for our experiments do not exist. It is not a contingent matter, however, that if we do find words to substitute for Yeats' they must differ in more than one respect from Yeats' words. Even this won't make the task of testing Stallworthy's claims impossible provided there is a sufficiently large stock of substitute rhyming words (though the relationship between the number we should need and the number of variables is a question we must leave to the mathematicians). And that there is not a sufficiently large number of such words is itself a contingent matter.

Still an impossibility is an impossibility. Why should we be concerned with what sort of impossibility we are confronted with here? The answer is that if it is only contingently impossible to test Stallworthy's claims, his claims are nonetheless claims, i.e. they are right or wrong, true or false, correct or incorrect, or whatever; it's just a contingent fact that we are unable to determine which. This in turn means that criticism of a sort which is logically similar to Stallworthy's may indeed be testable. Whether it is depends on the particular facts of the case. Now it may be true in general that criticism of this sort cannot be subjected to experimental testing. But experimental testing is not therefore inappropriate; it's just inapplicable.

But it is precisely this which may be questioned. The appropriateness of our treatment of Stallworthy depends on our having made appropriate reconstructions of explanations he does not in fact give us. And that he doesn't do this may itself be significant. It may be claimed that there are no missing explanations; that is to say, when Stallworthy says, 'We seem to detect a note of impatience in the facile rhyme, etc.' that is *all* he is saying. At least he is not committing himself to claims about the general connections or correlations between facility and impatience, except in as far as these connections can be seen to exist *a priori*. And his guarded claim that Yeats' slightly facile rhyme indicates impatience is, in the logician's sense, singular. Causal claims can be singular, and this one is, which explains why the first approach to Stallworthy's criticism was mistaken and irrelevant (cf. pp. 69–76). To treat Stallworthy's remark as inherently or implicitly general is like treating such remarks as 'That clock's striking reminds me that I must go' as implicitly general. But what we notice when we make such remarks is a particular causal connection. We do not have to establish, or believe in the existence of, a general connection between what we are reminded of and what has done the reminding, to say with justification and truth that the one thing reminds us of the other. Similarly, when the critic says that 'in the slightly facile rhyme, "embroideries/mythologies" one seems to detect a note of impatience', etc., he is not claiming that there is a general causal connection between rhymes of some sort and a suggestion of impatience. All he is saying is that he sees, or thinks that he sees, that this particular rhyme carries an air of impatience in this poem.

It might be felt that this interpretation of Stallworthy's critical remark is much more nearly correct than the previous one, but that a consequence of such an interpretation is that it, and similar remarks cannot be true or false, correct or mistaken, etc., but only persuasive or unpersuasive. But this does not follow. At least, remarks in which it is said that something has reminded one of something else can be mistaken or false. We are thinking here, not so much of situations in which, under pressure, perhaps from a third party, a man abandons such a remark in favour of another, 'Ah! Yes, you're right. It wasn't the clock, it was . . .', for if we are doubtful about the possibility of establishing that the first remark was correct, our doubts may carry over the second remark, which is of a logically similar sort to the first. It is the victim of a post-hypnotic suggestion who reveals that a man can be entirely ignorant of and mistaken about what reminds him of something else, and that the reason he gives is a mere rationalisation.

The victim of post-hypnotic suggestion reveals, somewhat paradoxically perhaps, that when we say, 'That reminds me . . .', we *are* saying something which is true or false. His being deceived shows that what a man says is not the criterion of what reminded him of whatever it was. But the existence of such odd cases does not show that in unexceptional cases a man might be wrong or mistaken about what has reminded him of what. A man could not be wrong, we might think, in the unexceptional case, not because it is logically impossible that he might be wrong, but because it is morally certain that he is right, just as, in most such cases, it is morally certain that he is in a better position to know what reminded him than anyone else. That is why we usually accept what he says.

If there is a logical truth here it is that in general a man knows what reminds him of whatever it is that he is reminded of, i.e. men are only mistaken in such matters on comparatively few occasions and not as a rule. For unless this were so, we should have no use for such remarks. We would treat them as we treat such impressionistic causal remarks as, 'Drinking tea is what has given me cancer of the stomach', or 'Drinking three pints of water every day is responsible for my great age and vigour'.

But of course, the explanation of our differing treatment of these remarks and the 'This reminds me . . . ' ones may simply be that we have not yet discovered that the latter are unreliable. If the suggestion that such a discovery might be made is intelligible, if it is logically possible that such a discovery might be made, then it is not a *logical* truth that in general men know what reminds them of what. But it may still be true that in general men do know this, and morally certain that they do.

Now how can we apply these remarks about 'This reminds me . . .' to Stallworthy's critical claim? Firstly, is there anything analogous to the victim of the post-hypnotic suggestion in criticism of this sort? That is to say, are we ever presented with attempts to locate and explain how a poem or a line in a poem produces an effect which can be proved to be false?

Sometimes we are. Thus, Johnson, while disdaining such trifling, technical matters[30] argues that the effect of certain passages of poetry, though commonly attributed to their sound or 'numbers', is in fact produced rather by their meaning.[31] He says, with appropriate caution, that 'the mind *often* governs the ear, and the sounds are estimated by their meaning'. (*Ibid*. our italics.) If we believe differently, and the critics have believed differently, we are wrong. Moreover, Johnson is able to show that we are wrong in particular cases by means of informal 'experiments'.

One of the most successful attempts has been to describe the labour of Sisyphus:

> With many a weary step, and many a groan,
> Up a (the) high hill he heaves a huge round stone;
> The huge round stone, resulting with a bound,
> Thunders impetuous down, and smoaks along the ground.

Who does not perceive the stone to move slowly upward, and roll violently back? But set the same numbers to another sense:

> While many a merry tale, and many a song,
> Cheer'd the rough road, we wish'd the rough road long.
> The rough road then, returning in a round,
> Mock'd our impatient steps, for all was fairly ground.

We have now surely lost much of the delay, and much of the rapidity.

Johnson has not shown that the length and rhythm of these lines play no part in determining their effect. If their length and rhythm were very different their effect might be different. He has shown, however, that they play a small part.

But could Stallworthy's attempt to locate what produces the feeling of impatience in Yeats' poem, and his attempt to explain how the rhyme does this, be refuted in such a decisive way? It would appear that it cannot. In this way it resembles the unexceptional 'This reminds me . . .' remarks. But although we usually accept the latter, and are right to do so, should we similarly accept the former remarks? The differences between the two sorts of cases suggest that we must be much more cautious with them.

In both cases, it might be said, we are, and can only be dealing with impressions. But in the cases of 'being reminded of' the claim made is an autobiographical one. The critical remark, in contrast, is intended to have a general validity —

any informed sensitive reader will detect the note of impatience in the facile half-rhyme.

Moreover, where we are dealing with cases in which a man says one thing reminds him of something else, the impression that this has happened is, characteristically, clear, strong and unambiguous. The phenomenological evidence can be so overwhelming that we may be unable to accept that we are wrong on such a matter no matter what the evidence against us. Some critical explanations logically akin to Stallworthy's may have a similar, immediate basis in our response to the work. But Stallworthy's remarks themselves do not have that kind of basis, not even for Stallworthy, for he only says that the facile half-rhyme *seems* to suggest impatience.

It might be thought that we can more easily accept Stallworthy's claim than an autobiographical analogue because he only speaks of what *seems* to be the case. But he is not really speaking of what seems to indicate impatience, i.e., he is not asserting that the facile rhyme (only) seems to indicate this, he is rather suggesting tentatively that it does indeed do this, and our questions is, 'Does the rhyme do this; and how?'

Another way in which it might be said that Stallworthy's remark is different from, and weaker than, 'This reminds me of that' claims is that it is *sensitising,* i.e. he is not claiming that a reader, or even an informed, sensitive reader *will* detect a note of impatience in the rhyme where this means that he will have done so prior to reading Stallworthy. He is only committed to the claim that, at any rate, *after* he has read Stallworthy's criticism the reader will do this. But this view of Stallworthy's criticism, though it has some foundation, makes it weaker than it really is. Stallworthy would surely expect other good readers to have noticed independently what he has noticed. If none had done this, we should all be that much more sceptical of what he says.

Mentioning the 'good', the 'sensitive, informed' reader indicates that Stallworthy's criticism also differs from a this-reminds-me claim in that it is normative. This means that a reader can fail to detect a note of impatience in the half-rhyme without thereby imperilling Stallworthy's claim. But this does not weaken, by reducing the substance of, what he is claiming unless a reader's lack of attention, or sensitivity, or scholar-ship, cannot be identified independently of his detecting of failing to detect the note of impatience. But even Stallworthy is unlikely to feel that a reader's having these desirable traits stands or falls with his detecting what Stallworthy thinks he detects here. The good reader is the reader who notices what is there to be noticed. What that means here is that persons who can read and understand — and also, perhaps, enjoy — poetry, and especially those who know their Yeats, will if they read this poem attentively, detect in the rhyme 'Embroideries/ mythologies' a note of impatience. At least, they will notice this after their attention has been drawn to it.

But *will* they? And, assuming that they do detect a note of impatience in the poem, is it the facile half-rhyme which conveys this impression? The ground-floor difficulty here is that even if we do get the impression of impatience on reading the poem, there is no strong, clear, unambiguous impression that the rhyme does this.

We can see that it may do it, since we can see that facility may be the product, and so a natural expression, of a man's impatience. But is it here? That is to say; does it give that impression here? And what that means, if the rhyme does not convey that impression immediately and independently of the rest of the poem, is: does the rhyme *help* to convey to us the feeling that Yeats was expressing an impatience with his old verse in this poem? To repeat: there is no phenomenological impression to guide us here — though even if there were, there would still be a problem, namely whether our impressions as to what is producing our responses are a good guide.

We might be tempted to say now that the rightness or wrongness of Stallworthy's claim can come to no more than our accepting it or not accepting it. This may be true sociologi-cally, as it were; it may indeed be the case that this is how this language game is played. But the explanation of why we proceed in this fashion may be, not that there is no truth or falsity here beyond our assent or dissent, but that either we simply don't bother to do the work necessary to test such claims when we do criticism, or that we don't do this because as a matter of fact we cannot do the work. The claims, though factual, are too elusive and complex to be put to the test. And this was our first view of the matter.

But isn't this last remark incompatible with the subsequent view that Stallworthy's claims, though causal, are singular? It is not if Stallworthy's claim that Yeats' facile rhyme indicates his impatience is only *epistemologically* singular. And this is indeed the case with this-reminds-me claims where the point can be more easily seen. When a man says, perhaps on seeing his coat lying over a chair, 'Oh, seeing that coat reminds me: I must go' he claims that he perceives, and so, *a fortiori* can perceive, a causal connection between two particular events. He is not committed to the claim that he has noticed in the past a general connection between seeing his coat and realising that it is time to go.[31] But he is committed to the view that his seeing his coat would remind him that he had to go in other situations if he were in the same state of mind, etc. And our view is, surely, that it is the features of the situation, or in the situation, which produce that response to seeing the coat, so that if the situation were repeated, he would again be reminded that he had to go. It is only if we believe that these causal claims are logically singular, so that they might be true even if repeating the situation did not produce the same response, that attempts to test such claims with experiments would be inappropriate.

But we don't believe this. When we say that 'This reminds me . . .' is a singular claim, we are noticing two facts about such remarks. The first is that we make such claims immediately without having noticed any general connection between events belonging to two classes. The second is that the events causally connected may be uniquely connected. But this does not mean that their causal connection does not depend on the general properties of the two things connected. All it means is that the combination of an event with such and such properties which produces an event with so and so properties is a unique combination.

That Stallworthy's remarks are indeed logically general can be more easily seen in connection with his mentioning the facility of Yeats' half-rhyme. To construe what he says here as absolutely singular is to interpret him as saying, 'It is the *facility-here*, the facility-of-this-rhyme-in-this-poem, which suggests Yeats' impatience. And it does this, not because the rhyme is facile, but because of this particular rhyme's particular facility'. It is not clear that such remarks make any sense; it is not clear to us that we have succeeded in articulating the problematic sense they would have to have if they really were logically singular. But if they are not singular, then such remarks are of a sort which can in principle be tested by experiment even if, owing to the complexities of these particular claims, they cannot in fact be tested.

In summary then: Stallworthy's critical remarks are not made on the basis of scientific investigation, they are particular observations. Nor can they be tested by experiment. They have an *a priori* plausibility because the very sense of the poem allows the interpretation that Yeats was expressing in it his dissatisfaction with his old verse and because facility can be seen as a sign of impatience. But whether this particular rhyme does contribute to that effect is not clear, nor is the manner in which it does so, if it does. It could contribute to this effect, and it only does do this if it has the effect on most informed, sensitive readers of the poem. But that it does so is not determined by what they say (for, apart from sceptical difficulties, the phenomenological evidence is inconclusive here), though in fact what they say will determine whether Stallworthy's criticism is accepted or rejected.

3 The logical richness of criticism: an analysis of Ricks on Tennyson

Partly because we wished to demonstrate its multifariousness, partly because criticism is complex and our investigations are analytic, we have so far looked at a variety of examples but each has rarely been more than a few sentences long or, if longer, we have usually concentrated on just one issue raised by the longer piece. So our examples are short, and criticism is characteristically much more sustained. Conversely, our analyses are minute and long, so that readers, especially critics, are likely to feel that what we have had to say about our examples does not capture, and, therefore, can only misrepresent, the experience of reading criticism.

Now this second point can be dealt with fairly easily: the ease and speed with which a professional reads something is no certain guide either to its complexity or even to the complexity of his response to it. Indeed it can be misleading, and we have tried to show in the last chapters how, for example, a critic may treat difficult and elusive matters informally and intuitively.

The first objection raises a practical problem: anything like a comprehensive analytic discussion of a sustained piece of criticism, especially if the criticism is itself analytic or practical, is almost bound to be impossibly long, i.e. unreadable and unpublishable.[1]

We cannot entirely solve this problem but by now, if Christopher Ricks does have a characteristic approach to the business of criticism, this will be familiar to our readers. So in this chapter we try to give a more comprehensive account of the nature of, and problems raised by a longer piece of his work. Our primary aim is to demonstrate the enormous logical richness— and, very often, the elusiveness— of criticism.

In doing this we also hope to correct a whole series of mistakes made by other philosophers of criticism. We shall argue that certain of the remarks in the piece of criticism which follows are not only 'descriptive' but 'interpretative' and

84

'evaluative', and that sometimes these elements can scarcely be separated. Indeed the ways in which they are brought together varies in different remarks and sometimes it cannot be said how they are conjoined. We shall try to show that no monolithic claim can be made about interpretative judgements that they are never true or false, or about descriptive ones that they are always true or false;[2] and, again, that critical judgements often have a causal dimension.[3] We are especially interested in showing the points at, and ways in which critical remarks become untestable; and note that there is often little correspondence between the rhetoric of certain passages in this piece, in particular the tone of confidence adopted, and the problematic status of what is being claimed. This suggests that the author is not always aware of the dubiety of what he is saying, or is responding to a half-awareness with insistence; thus it is not only philosophers of criticism that we seek to correct. In either case we are left with the questions: is the interesting and sometimes persuasive remark made by the critic true, and how could we test this? And if this attitude sometimes seems inappropriate, why is this so?

We have chosen Ricks' criticism of a short poem embedded in Tennyson's *In Memoriam*.[4] (We also allude to other works for purposes of comparison.) We should explain that we discuss Ricks so much because he is a fine critic, a good representative of the modern school of practical critics, but one whose very qualities — well represented in this passage — raise problems about what he has to say.

The poem that follows is a section from Tennyson's *In Memoriam* (1850), a sequence which he wrote on the death of his friend, Arthur Hallam. This particular section has been picked out by T.S. Eliot as one of Tennyson's greatest poems. That it deals with an important and enduring subject can hardly be doubted — but how does Tennyson make his poem novel as well as natural? What is there in its structure and its detail that makes the poem impinge on the reader's mind and heart?

> Dark house, by which once more I stand
>   Here in the long unlovely street,
>   Doors, where my heart was used to beat
> So quickly, waiting for a hand.

> A hand that can be clasp'd no more—
>   Behold me, for I cannot sleep,
>   And like a guilty thing I creep
> At earliest morning to the door.
>
> He is not here; but far away
>   The noise of life begins again,
>   And ghastly thro' the drizzling rain
> On the bald streets breaks the blank day.

First there is the poignant disparity between the tragic grief of the theme and the simple casualness of the anecdote. In one sense it is, after all, a poem about paying a social call, about asking if someone is in and being told, almost casually, 'he is not here'. Our shock is at the gap between what such a disappointment ordinarily means and what the disappointment is here. Hallam is not simply out, he is dead. And Tennyson fixes on us a sense of the appalling ordinariness of death precisely by making his poem into a grim parody of a simple incident like paying a call. The tragic subject gives the poem dignity and weight; the simple anecdote saves that dignity from becoming pompous or ponderous. We are all disappointed to find that a friend is out — but how much more sweeps in on this particular moment of loss!

Second, there is the mild surprise that comes of the fact — completely convincing as soon as one is told of it by the poem— that the surviving friend and the London scene itself are even more dead then the departed friend, that it is the survivor who really feels the numbness of death. The speaker is like a ghost who 'cannot sleep', haunting— in both senses of the word— the place where his friend has lived. He is 'like a guilty thing' — a phrase which encompasses two effects. One, it pinpoints that strange quirk of feeling by which the one who is left alive feels somehow guilty— the dead friend seems somehow so much worthier than oneself, and it is as if in staying alive one is taking unfair advantage of the arbitrariness and injustice of life and death. Second, the phrase echoes a famous moment in *Hamlet*, when the ghost of Hamlet's father 'started like a guilty thing' and faded at the crowing of the cock. Tennyson's use of the allusion is wonderfully apt; for any reader who takes the point, there is manifested in the poem a sense not only that the speaker is like the ghost, but also of another world of tragedy and death. And yet the reader who misses the allusion will not find Tennyson's line empty of meaning— it makes an acute and vivid psychological point about the sense of guilt. In other words, the line does not *depend*, does not stake everything, on our recognizing the allusion; it hopes, but it does not insist, that we will. And it is the same with a further allusion that is carried by the same phrase, a phrase which Wordsworth had incorporated in his *Ode: Intimations of Immortality* (notice Wordsworth's title and theme, and its relation to Tennyson's):

Blank misgivings of a Creature
Moving about in worlds not realized,
High instincts, before which our mortal Nature
Did tremble like a guilty Thing surprized . . .

Once again Tennyson is not demanding that we take his allusion, but his line will be the richer if we do.

The poem makes use, then, of the slight but telling surprise that comes of treating what survives as if it were the real victim of death (I am the one who is really dead, in being deprived of him). There is the same twisting of expectation, the same ability to make a poem on this oldest of subjects something new and unique, in the close of the poem. We are used to associating night with despair, and the coming of dawn with new hope. But what do we find?

And ghastly thro' the drizzling rain
On the bald street breaks the blank day.

'Ghastly' means not just 'horrifying', but 'ghostly'; the dictionary gives for *ghastly* 'like a spectre or dead body', so that the dawn itself comes like a ghost (in the ordinary way, a ghost flees at the coming of the dawn, as Hamlet's father did). The street is 'bald' in its ugliness, in its unvarnished truth, and in being suddenly like an ageing person. The day is blank both in being desolately vacant and in being white — a poem by James Thomson mentioned 'Blank, in the leaden-coloured east, the moon'. The heavy stresses of the last line bring great force on to the word 'breaks' so that we really do think of it, not just with the commonplace acceptance of 'day-break', but as something actually breaking; day breaks 'on the bald street' as something fragile shatters on something stony, or as a heart breaks. Yet the poem, despite its reversal of expectation (the survivor is a ghost, the coming of dawn intensifies the sense of loss), does not simply succumb to despair or pessimism. There is, even in those closing lines, a sense of an undercurrent that is striving to run the other way. After all, day does break; the poem does begin with the word 'Dark' and end with the word 'day'; and the 'noise of life' does begin again even though from one point of view that simply strengthens the sense of loss. Even the stanza-form of the poem is one that beautifully poises hope against despair, affirmation against loss. The rhymes (stand/street/beat/hand) have the form *abba*; that is, they rise in the middle of each stanza to a strong conjunction, and then fade away with the last line — though not into utter hopelessness, because there is an answering rhyme. But it is a distant rhyme and a distant hope — it is only faintly that the necessary rhyme-word from the first line of the stanza can still sound in our heads. The *abba* stanza was perfectly adapted to the ebbing and flowing of Tennyson's grief and hope.

But there is a third implicit idea which controls the poem; the idea that the speaker is standing not just before Hallam's house, but before Hallam's dead body. The idea is a subterranean one in the poem, and by no means obtrusive, but it seems to me responsible for a great deal of the quiet force of the lines. What kind of substantiation might there be for the critic here? For one thing, there is a very ancient tradition, especially in funeral elegy, which sees the body as a kind of house. The Anglo-Saxon word for a body was indeed *ban-hus*, bone-house, and the idea is perfectly apt to Christian beliefs about the freedom attained by the soul when the body dies. The dead body would then be a 'dark house'. But not only is there the evidence of a well-known tradition, there is evidence that Tennyson himself made use of the tradition. Three years before the death of Hallam, Tennyson published a poem, called *The Deserted House*, which deals explicitly with the feelings of a man who gazes at a dead body and imagines it as a house, now deserted, from which the soul has departed to heaven. Moreover, the climax of the earlier poem is a stanza which resembles the *In Memoriam* stanza form, a stanza which many readers of Tennyson would vaguely attribute to *In Memoriam* itself:

> Close the door, the shutters close,
>   Or thro' the windows we shall see
>   The nakedness and vacancy
> Of the dark deserted house.

'The dark deserted house' (compare 'Dark house') is the dead body, its eyes staring like windows that must now be closed. The evidence of this earlier poem by Tennyson seems to me to support the idea that in 'Dark house' there is a strong though tacit suggestion that the speaker is standing before the corpse of his friend as well as before the house. Which is why we find that the speaker does in fact address the house — not a farfetched exclamation, but a natural relapse into trying to speak to the dead body: 'Dark house . . . Behold me'. Behold me? Its windows are the eyes of a corpse.

As with any great poem, there are a hundred other points of detail which call for attention, but enough has perhaps been said to show just how this particular poem combines novelty and nature, and lifts itself above the ruck of funeral elegies which never persuade us of any heartfelt grief. Tennyson's short poem has the weight appropriate to its huge subject, because it works on us — partly directly and partly by stealth — with three dignified surprises: it combines the mystery of death with the ordinariness of a social call; it gives the sense that it is we, who are alive, who are really the dead; and it stands before a house which is at the same time, with a poetic double exposure, a corpse.

Firstly, when Ricks mentions 'the poignant disparity between the tragic grief of the theme and the simple casualness of the anecdote', this could be said to be any or all of the following; a description of one aspect of the theme of the poem, of what it is about (the grief felt by Tennyson at the loss of his friend, and its outward expression in the rather ordinary occasion of his visiting his friend's house); an interpretation of the relationship between these two elements in the theme (Ricks sees a disparity between them, where others might feel too little distinction, or else a sense of complete disconnection); an assessment of the effect this has on the mood of the poem (Ricks feels a mood of poignancy, where others might feel bathos), which is itself close to an evaluation of what the poem achieves (namely poignancy), and a strong indication of Ricks' response to the poem; and the suggestion, at least, of an explanation of how the poignancy is achieved, namely through the 'disparity between the tragic grief of the theme and the simple casualness of the anecdote'— although it is just possible that Ricks may merely be saying that there is a disparity and it is poignant, that is without any suggestion that it is poignant in virtue of its disparity. This interfusion of different aspects of critical comment continues throughout Ricks' analysis. Sometimes the fusion is so complete that we scarcely notice that more than one claim is being made.

Ricks goes on to say that 'there is the mild surprise that comes of the fact— completely convincing as soon as one is told of it by the poem — that the surviving friend and the London scene itself are even more dead that the departed friend, that it is the survivor who really feels the numbness of death'. In spite of Ricks' authoritative grammar and phraseology here, the poem does not tell us, literally or explicitly anyway, that this is the case; and what Ricks intends with this paradoxical metaphor is not entirely clear. Is the narrator 'numb' in the sense of not fully understanding his friend's death until the late realisation of 'He is not here'? It might equally well be argued that that phrase sums up the feeling of change since his friend's death, a change explored in the previous two stanzas. Perhaps *that* is Ricks' claim, and he is using numbness loosely to suggest loss — it is the survivor who feels the blankness, the lack of the friend's presence, which the dead man himself cannot feel.

If it is, Ricks is at the least confused, speaking of the narrator as being '*more* dead' than the departed friend; and his metaphor confuses rather than clarifies, for terms like 'numb' and 'dead' run against the pain of loss which is to be found in the poem as well as the blankness ('I cannot sleep, And like a guilty thing I creep At earliest morning to the door' suggests that hyper-awareness of insomnia, an obsessive remembering of his friend's death). The second part of the claim, that the London scene is 'more dead than the departed friend', might also be disputed for the same reasons; what of 'the noise of life begins again'?

So what is presented as 'the fact' is seen to be a complex of claims the identities of which are not fully specified, and those we've looked at so far are problematic; and on these Ricks rests two further claims which he presents with equal certainty. One is about the effect on the reader of this feature of the poem, which Ricks tells us is one of 'mild surprise', and which he later cites as contributing to the originality and novelty of the treatment of a well-worn subject; and one with an evaluative dimension, that this 'fact' is made 'completely convincing' by Tennyson, the implication being that he has skilfully made us aware of an important truth.

All of these claims are embedded in a sentence which at first has every appearance of giving a description of the literal meaning of part of the poem. Thus we see the different dimensions of critical comment may be not just compressed and interfused; on occasions different kinds of claim, which depend for their validity on a chain of acceptance, are submerged beneath one apparently single, acceptable claim. In this way a piece of criticism can work on us without our being fully aware of the different dimensions concealed in it, or of the nature of the connections between them.

What we have said so far suggests that if we could tease out the various things that the critic does, sometimes in a single sentence, and establish the logical relationships between these various things, we should get a clear picture of what he is doing. But the terms we use in our analysis are themselves not univocal. Thus there is a strong suggestion in the preceding discussion that a critical claim is interpretative when it is about meaning in some way but is contestable, or problematic. But 'meaning' itself has many meanings, which allows as a possibility what is a fact, *viz.*, that interpretative issues are enormously heterogeneous. And the banality, for example, that *Animal Farm* is about Stalinism (which does not preclude its being about other things as well) shows that not all interpretative claims are problematic.[5]

Within Ricks' piece there are many different sorts of interpretative claim. The first which might be interpretative is that 'in one sense' the poem is 'about paying a social call'. This first example seems borderline as to whether it is interpretative or not, for although it is about what the poem is about, the poem seems to say what it is about. However, Ricks goes on to modify this claim by restating it; the poem, he says, is 'a grim parody . . . of paying a call'. The claim about literal meaning has become one about mood and attitude.

Ricks' next and clearly interpretative claim, just discussed, is that the surviving friend is more dead that the one who has died. Ricks presents this and his first claim as being of a sort, i.e. equally certain, but as we have shown his second claim is dubious. Furthermore, the grounds he offers for it are themselves contestable interpretative claims, one about the nature of the 'guilt' mentioned, and two involving awareness of literary allusions — a contentious area, as Ricks himself recognises in marking these as optional elements in our interpretation.

Ricks' next interpretative claim, that the combination of the coming of dawn with the continuing mood of depression produces a reversal of expectation, depends among other things on a new factor, the symbolic connotations which a word characteristically has. It is followed by a claim of a similar sort, that nevertheless, owing to other features in this section from *In Memoriam*, there is a slight lightening of the mood. Ricks sees these interpretative claims as requiring argument, and he is right about this, but in these cases one would be more inclined to accept the basis for the claim rather than the claims themselves.

His final interpretative claim is that the 'dark house' is a symbol for Hallam's body. He sees this as being even more elusive, and again he is right. For in his previous claims he did not have to prove the symbolic connotations of 'day' and 'dark' which were part of his supporting argument: but 'house' doesn't have any such pervasive or natural symbolic connotations. This is a claim which has to be proved about a particular case, yet Ricks has to do this by going outside the poem.

Such a brief comparison of interpretative remarks, even though it contains no attempt to resolve any of the problems raised by each, is enough to show that any worthwhile discussion of interpretation in criticism has to be of particular cases. And this is illustrative of similar points, which could be made about evaluation, description, etc.

Let us now examine the logical relationships between and indeed within various remarks of Ricks.

In our previous discussion of the sentence containing the phrase 'poignant disparity' we demonstrated that Ricks was making a variety of points which are brought together in the phrase but only, as it were, physically, almost by the conjunction of 'poignant' and 'disparity'. Now this is a rhetorically effective way of connecting claims in our minds, for it presents them all together and conceals the fact that more than one claim is being made. But a consequence of this stylistic device is that if we become sceptical of what the critic has to say, since he hasn't made any attempt to connect them they will seem to fall apart.[6] Similar points could be made about Ricks' use of 'quiet force'.

In contrast there are other places where Ricks does try to give, or at least suggest, an account of the relationship between one claim and another. He mentions in the course of his analysis that the rhyme scheme is abba (this is incontrovertible of course, and if we wanted to save 'description' for what was incontrovertible then it should be saved for matters of this sort) and he continues, as though making clear this descriptive claim: 'that is, they[the rhymes] rise in the middle of each stanza to a strong conjunction and then fade away with the last line'. But this is not just an alternative description of the rhyme scheme; it is that, plus a characterisation of the feeling which is embodied in and conveyed by the rhyme scheme. And Ricks claims that this feeling contributes to and is constitutive of the particular ebbing and flowing of feeling (namely of Tennyson's grief and hope) which in his view is expressed in this section of *In Memoriam*. So we have a descriptive claim, that the rhyme scheme is abba; an interpretative claim, that these lines express the ebbing and flowing of Tennyson's grief and hope; and a (partial) explanation of how that effect is achieved, namely through the abba rhyme scheme.[7]

What, then, is the relationship between the descriptive and interpretative claims? The first is undeniable; the second is not, and some of us feel it to be false. And since there is no incoherence in supposing that the second is false while the first is true, the first can't entail the second — nor presumably would Ricks think it did. Conversely, there is nothing incoherent in the supposition that if — apparently *per impossibile* — Tennyson's lines did not conform to this rhyme scheme they would not express the ebb and flow of his hope and grief.

Perhaps translation into a foreign language might provide a not unreal and not too unfair test, but again, to say this is to say that there is no incoherence in the supposition that the lines might convey this feeling and yet not exhibit the abba rhyme scheme.

It is tempting to infer that since there is no entailment relationship between these claims their relationship cannot be logical and so must be empirical and indeed causal, if it exists at all. But this is too quick. The relationship might be a logical one without being a matter of entailment. For example a man could be a good footballer without being able to run fast, conversely, he might be able to run fast and be no good at football, but part of a man's footballing ability, perhaps his chief virtue, might be his great speed, and being very fast is constitutive of the ideal footballer.

What would be an analogous claim here? It is very difficult to say, but presumably it would be something like this; an abba rhyme scheme is, in poetry at any rate, constitutive, if not of the ebbing and flowing of feeling itself, of its expression. Although we should remind ourselves that this claim differs from the analogous case about the ideal footballer, and is weaker, i.e. claims less than that, for it does not rule out the possibility that other rhyme schemes could also be perfectly adapted to the expression of the ebbing and flowing of feeling in poetry such as abbcca, abccba, and so on.)

But do we have a concept, or, less pretentiously, an (any) idea of what, in poetry, would be involved in the ideal expression of the ebb and flow of feeling? If we do, does it include the abba rhyme scheme, at least at such times in the development of poetry when it has been possible to make use of it? Ricks may be committing himself to affirmative answers to both of these questions when he concludes 'the abba stanza was perfectly adapted to the ebbing and flowing of Tennyson's grief and hope'. But he may not be and even if he were it would be impossible to say whether he was right.

Another possibility is that the claim he is making, in so far as it can be assigned a status, is an empirical, causal one. If the claim is a causal one, is it true? The fact that the rhyme scheme is abba, even together with the truth of Ricks' interpretative claim, is insufficient to establish that the rhyme scheme is instrumental in producing the ebbing and flowing of feeling in the verse. It could be, but there is no conclusive experimental way of putting such a claim to the test. For even a translation into a foreign language which preserved the sense of Tennyson's lines but which altered their rhyme scheme would ineluctably introduce other differences which could explain why the ebbing and flowing of feeling either was preserved or disappeared.

A critic might feel that this was somehow too quick a way of dealing with the so-called causal view of his explanation, which anyway got it wrong and misrepresented it. He might say that in the case of this poem there simply is a *fit* between the rhyme scheme and the ebbing and flowing of emotion in the poem. This is a subtle claim which needs spelling out, but what is being suggested is roughly this: the strong rhyme, bb matches the predominant feeling, which is grief, and its central position in the stanza matches and reinforces the rising to a peak of that grief: and the rhyme in the final line answers that in the first, but only distantly and so weakly, and thus matches the faint return of hope.

If we were to object to this on the grounds that such a rhyme scheme might fit as well or fit better, a poem in which the predominant feeling was one of hope, but tinged with despondency (the 'strong conjunction' ought to sound uplifting), the critic would have no need to deny this. His claim is merely that the strong rhyme matches with whatever the predominant feeling happens to be.

If we objected that the sense of the middle two lines in each particular stanza of this section of *In Memoriam* is no more concerned with expressing grief than that of the first and last lines, the critic's reply would be that the matching is not of that close and indeed rather crude sort. The ebbing and flowing of feeling is an overall one; the rhymes match, echo, and reinforce it in each stanza.

Now it cannot be denied that we can see some kind of weak congruity between the rhyme pattern and the ebb and flow of feeling (assuming as we are that there is such a feeling in the poem). But the main difficulty seems to be that perceived congruities of this tenuous sort can be seen almost anywhere. Suppose, for instance, we have a rhyme scheme aaaa; could this not match, and so echo and reinforce, the feelings expressed in a poem which are initially feelings of triumph, which are gradually replaced by those of desperation, which in turn are overcome by a final triumph matched, echoed and reinforced by the triumphant closing rhyme in each stanza? The second difficulty is this: given that there is a congruity between the rhyme scheme and the progression of feeling, does the former not merely match but reinforce the latter? We are back again to a causal claim.

But the critic may feel that what he has to say is still misrepresented. For the reinforcing effect of the rhymes' matching the feeling is not an *inference* from the matching but is *constituted* by it. To perceive the fit is to perceive the reinforcing. Thus experiment is otiose.

But the mere assertion of an identity cannot create one, and even if we concede the existence of the congruity we still want to know if it does any work, and this is a causal question. Now it may very well be that the critic feels that there is no need to ask this question because — and he is right in this — he sees the matching not as something fortuitous and accidental but as a device used by the writer to gain some effect. (To try to throw some light on the critic's claim here; if we see a man waving his arms about as we drive along a road we are not likely to stop unless we think that he is trying to wave us down, trying to make us stop by waving his arms. And if we realize that that is what he is doing he may stop us. To ignore this dimension of a literary device would be like treating the movements of the man's arms like the shaking of a tree's branches.)

Again, we cannot deny the truth of what the critic says; but again we cannot overlook the question, does the device succeed? The existence of the congruity, even together with its being intended, does not ensure that the rhyme scheme either adds to the ebb and flow of feeling in the poetry or adds to our awareness of it. Whether it does in a case of this sort where the congruity is so attenuated (and the interpretative claim about the feeling is itself dubious) remains then an ingenious hypothesis but one we could not test.

Mentioning the word 'device' suggests yet a fourth possible account of the relationship between such things as rhyme schemes and the feeling expressed in verse, though we mention it only to introduce a fifth. It could be that there is a conventional relationship between rhyme schemes and the emotions expressed in poetry. Now such conventions do not exist in English poetry — at least not in relation to rhyme scheme alone[8] — though of course the expression of emotion in poetry is highly stylised. Moreover, even if they did exist, a writer could not be certain that merely by making use of some such convention he would succeed in creating the effect he desired.

However, if for whatever reason, writers, critics or their readers believed that, in some way or other, certain rhyme schemes *did* express certain emotions, then they would tend to do so. The belief that they do this, accepting that they do it, would lead to their doing it. *In this way a critic if he is sufficiently persuasive or respected may create the substantive truth of the claims he makes.*

So it is unclear what kind of relationship Ricks thinks exists between the two claims (and hence what kind of explanation he is essaying), and it is unclear whether, whatever sort of relationship he thinks it is, it obtains, but it is clear that it would be as good as impossible to establish that it did obtain.

Given that Ricks' explanation is virtually untestable and is in any case an incomplete, partial explanation[9], what can it achieve? It can only draw our attention to something in the poem which may — or may not — contribute to the ebbing and flowing of feeling in the poem. Whether it does so contribute or not, we really cannot say.[10] Ricks treats both the interpretative claim and the explanatory one as unproblematic, and so he seems to be attempting something like a mere investigation into the mechanics of the poetry. But let us suppose that the interpretative claim is itself dubious, and that the critic realises this in some way, or appreciates that possibility; then the *role* of the explanation will be of a rather different sort. It does not merely provide a technical account of how in part the ebb and flow of feeling in the poetry is produced or reinforced, or draw our attention to a device whose effect is to make us more aware of the ebb and flow of feeling. Its role is to give support to the interpretative claim, i.e. to make it more likely and so more acceptable.

It would do this if it could be shown to be true, and even if it couldn't be shown to be true but were merely inherently plausible, it would lend plausibility to the interpretative claim.[11] Of course, a claim that the rhyme scheme helps to produce, reinforce or heighten our awareness simply of an ebbing and flowing of feeling in the poetry, even if it could be shown to be true or were inherently plausible, wouldn't make the particular version of the interpretative claim which is Ricks' (that there is an ebbing and flowing of *grief* and *hope*) more likely than other versions of that interpretative claim, unless we knew what the predominant feeling was.

A critic might well feel, especially after reading this kind of analysis, that really it doesn't matter what sort of explanation he is essaying or how it works, the important thing is that it works, because the important thing is the interpretative claim. But presumably the interpretative claim is important because it is true and it gives insight, that is its being accepted by a reader signifies his achieving an awareness, a knowledge that he had lacked. But it is only if it does do this, and does so unproblematically, that we might sympathise with the critic's reaction. (But how could it be unproblematic in a case of this sort? He may be certain he has insight, but has he?) And even then, if his reader is being persuaded to the apprehension of a truth by methods that are not what they appear to be, indeed by mere rhetoric, an outsider at any rate might feel that it is important to point this out.

So far, then, we have construed Ricks as offering an untestable hypothesis about what is (partially) responsible in the sense for the ebb and flow of feeling he detects there, clothed in a specious verbal certainty.

But to throw more light on the nature of Ricks' argument, and its point, let us suppose that another critic disagrees with his *interpretative* claim. He feels not so much the ebbing and flowing of Tennyson's grief and hope in the lines but — and sometimes the critic's first task is to try to characterise more precisely what he does feel — the flowing, and more strongly the ebbing of Tennyson's inspiration. He feels despair in the lines, but not the despair apprehended by Ricks. He too casts about for something in the poetry which may have helped to create the laboured feeling of the verse which he detects, and it occurs to him that one thing that may have helped to create it is precisely the abba rhyme scheme. The return to the rhyme of the first line in the final line of each stanza, conveys desperation and weariness rather than a return of hope.

Here, again, we have an untestable hypothesis, but a rival one to Ricks', to explain a rival interpretation. Yet the explanation could be right and indeed it seems as inherently plausible as Ricks'; moreover, it could be right even if Ricks' claim were also right. That is, the critic here could be right in suspecting that one feature of the poem which helps to contribute to *his* feeling that it is laboured is the rhyme scheme. For given a prior view that Tennyson's poetry tends to be laboured, the rhyme scheme which may contribute to the ebbing and flowing of feeling which Ricks detects may indeed for the rival critic contribute to its feeling laboured. And if the critic were right about this, he wouldn't be inventing his view of the poetry or pretending that something was involved in creating that view which in fact was not involved in doing so. His only pretence or mistake might lie in his thinking that he knew that the rhyme had played a role here, and in presenting his claim as though it were knowledge. It is only in that way and to that extent that he, like Ricks, would be rationalising.

So apparently we could have two untestable hypotheses about how two rival interpretations might have been produced, which it would seem do not threaten each other even though they both refer to the same feature in the work to explain the different responses, except to the extent that they make the reader realise that there is more than one possible interpretation of the poem, and so threaten the appearance of certainty, of rightness, which each critic adopts and which is, of course, unwarranted.

Yet we cannot forbear to ask at this point, 'But who is right?' and this is not simply a question about which explanation is right. And with this question a dimension of critical arguments of this sort, their nature and their point, starts to become visible— the normative dimension.

What this dimension is can be made clearer if we imagine yet a third critic, who says, for example, that the feeling conveyed by the poem for him is one of extreme happiness, and that this is created by the abba rhyme scheme. Our immediate reaction here is, 'Nonsense!'. But he may reply that he has a very odd sensibility. He reacts so strongly to this particular rhyme scheme that its presence is sufficient in the poem for the poem to strike him as a happy one. Of course, he may be pretending or he might be sincere yet mistaken. But simply because the claim he makes is such a strong one it can be put to the test, and on being put to the test it might turn out to be right. But the fact that his explanation of his response can be shown to be right here has no effect other than to strengthen our view that his response is itself a bizarre one. It certainly does not threaten Ricks' view in any way.

It may now be beginning to look as if we have been looking at Ricks' argument in a wrong way, and perhaps, if faced with the case of the third critic, he himself might point out, with some impatience, that discovering what produces his response is not what a critic is trying to do. He is not trying to give a quasi-scientific explanation of certain phenomenological data, namely how he responds, he is rather trying to make clearer, more intelligible, more acceptable, trying to justify his interpretation. His argument is not so much that the poem does in fact convey a certain feeling in a certain way, but that it should do so and will do so for the sensitive reader.

Someone in Ricks' position might underline his point here with an analogy. He might say: 'I might offer as an explanation for my dislike of a man that he is mean. It may not be clear that his being mean in fact played a part in determining my attitude to him (clearly it played no part if he was mean but I was unaware of it, so that my claim that he was mean was fortuitously correct. Though it would not always be easy to determine in a case of this sort whether I was aware that he was mean.) But if what is at issue is not *whether* he is dislikeable, i.e. worthy of dislike, the fact — given that it is a fact — that I was not aware of this, or even the fact that I was aware of it but it did not matter to me, that is it played no part in determining my attitude, has no tendency to undermine the claim that he is dislikeable because he is mean. Likewise', he might continue, 'even if the abba rhyme scheme in fact played no part in determining my response to the poem, but was something I noticed only after I started to try to justify, explain, make intelligible, my feelings about it; its status as a reason for, a partial justification of, my interpretation of the poem is not impugned.'

So now it seems that we should not approach claims such as Ricks' as untestable impressionistic hypotheses about what may have produced the critic's response, but rather as claims about how one should respond to the work, and why one should, that is, how certain features of the work should affect one.

But there are two difficulties here. Firstly, meanness is *per se* dislikeable. But is it similarly the case that an abba rhyme scheme *should* heighten or reinforce or produce an ebbing and flowing of feeling in poetry — even supposing that we knew that in the case of someone like Ricks it does in fact do this? And that, of course, remains a difficulty, namely that even for someone like Ricks we cannot tell, and he cannot know, that what he claims ought to reinforce, heighten or produce an ebbing and flowing of feeling in this poem, does in fact do so for him.[12]

So Ricks' argument is, as is characteristic of criticism, a normative one; but this, far from ruling out its causal dimension — as some commentators have seemed to think — presupposes and requires it.

The normative dimension of Ricks' claim requires the truth of the causal one, which however does not generate the former. And this is not because the causal claim is so elusive. For example, a man might claim that he finds any poem written in heroic couplets therefore funny,[14] and some simple, though necessarily fairly extended and tedious experiment, could confirm that he was right. But of course this would not demonstrate that he was right in thinking any particular poem funny, and funny because of its being in heroic couplets. So now we touch on the large question: how do we justify normative judgements in criticism?

The response of the man in our example is aberrant, and the word itself reminds us that we tend to assess such responses by measuring them against the norm, the common response of readers of poetry, which springs from a shared sensibility in these readers. Moreover, this common sensibility is necessary to art; the artist's task would be impossible if he could not rely to some extent on the knowledge that certain features will produce certain effects, certain responses. He would not be able to attempt anything which did not depend entirely on the literal sense; and this would make nonsense of the art of poetry. (And of course these connections between certain features and their effects are themselves strengthened by the artist's exploitation of them.) So any response which deviates too far from the common one will raise a problem.

The man's response in our example is doubly aberrant. It is massive and undiscriminating. The metrical form is in itself sufficient to determine his reaction, regardless of anything else in the work. So that even if he read a heroic couplet which made no sense he would find it funny — nothing else counts for him in a case of this sort. But even if the heroic couplet were not sufficient for his amusement, he would still be aberrant in associating the heroic couplet with what is funny. For there is no generally felt connection between the heroic couplet and what is funny, and in the absence of any account on his part as to why he finds it funny, his response is brute, unintelligible, eccentric, and destructive (destructive in that it would usually interfere with his appreciation of what a poet was trying to do, and perhaps succeeding in doing, for many readers). Even if he were to attempt some explanation and justification for his peculiarity, this consequence of his aberrance would remain.

Of course, we can think of particular examples where the heroic couplet might strike us as funny — for example, Pope's 'Rape of the Lock' (or where the heroic mode is employed, as in Gray's 'On a Favourite Cat, Drowned in a Tub of Gold Fishes'). But these cases are funny, partly, precisely because of the incongruity which depends on the generally felt connection between the heroic couplet and matters which are heroic.[15]

Where such a connection does exist, as it seems to here, on what is it based? Why is there a connection between the heroic metre and heroic matters? Aristotle felt it to be a natural connection. He described the heroic hexameter (in Greek poetry the heroic measure was 12-syllable; in English it is 10-syllable) as the 'right metre' for epic. It

has the greatest weight and stability . . . and so no one has ever written a poem on the grand scale in any other metre than the heroic measure; as I have said, Nature herself teaches us to choose the right metre for our purpose.[16]

But whether Aristotle is right or not and whatever the original reason for choosing the heroic hexameter for the epic (that is, whatever made it appropriate — even supposing that it was), the fact that it had been chosen and epic poets had used it established a connection, which must have become a powerful factor in determining how a man wrote (about heroic matters), and how a reader reacted.

Yet such connections are not constant or invulnerable, which suggests that they're not — *tout court* anyway — 'natural', or if in some way they are, they may be superseded by other elements in our relationship with works of art (which is one reason why a science of response of works of art would be more difficult than a science of natural phenomena). This particular connection has collapsed in the course of the history of poetry. For a contemporary poem in heroic metre, far from rousing associations with the heroic, would probably strike us as absurd — and, ironically, the more so if the poet were dealing with heroic matters. In fact if we adjust our example somewhat, if, say, the man does not find the heroic couplet *per se* funny but simply tending towards the ludicrous (so that the sense *could* overwhelm his tendency to react in that way), we would no longer have an imaginary eccentric, but a present-day reader reacting to a contemporary poem written in traditional epic style. Of course such a reaction would be limited to contemporary poetry, and that may be because the notion of the heroic as a contemporary subject is absurd. This second reader certainly would not find anything inherently ludicrous in a heroic hexameter from Homer, and its heroic associations would seem perfectly appropriate.[17] But our eccentric would find Homer's lines equally ludicrous.

But our example may seem to critics so extreme as to be unreal and unilluminating. So let us look at a more realistic case. One man reads some lines of Keats', comments on the mellifluous sound of the poetry, and attributes this to the abundance of 'l' and 'r' sounds in the lines.[18] Another man finds that these lines create not a mellifluous impression, but one of sharpness and harshness and again he attributes this to the 'l' and 'r' sounds. Surely the first man's response is the right one, in that there does seem to be a pervasive connection between 'l' and 'r' sounds and an effect of liquidity and fluency; and, rightly or wrongly, we think we can give some account of why this connection exists, just as we feel we can give an account of why it is generally felt that Italian, say, is a mellifluous language and German a harsh, unmusical one. The first man's response is the common one, and no doubt the one which Keats actually intended — he may have deliberately used words with 'l' and 'r' sounds to achieve such an effect. Of course, the sense will have lent something here. But even if we perform an experiment and create a line full of 'l' and 'r' sounds which make no sense, the impression is still likely to be one of fluency, though an undirected fluency it is true. In a case of this sort, the second man's response is of such a sort that it is not only aberrant, but unintelligible and wrong.

So deciding what response a certain technical feature should arouse can be a very straightforward matter, it can simply be a matter of knowing the effect it has on the average sensitive man, and in certain cases, we have shown, this can be tested. (It is interesting, too, that in the example just discussed we do not find it absurd that a line of nonsense should still have a certain effect, one of fluency and liquidity, because of a certain feature, whereas in the previous example it was clearly absurd that heroic couplets should be *per se* funny. Is this the difference between connections which have a natural basis and those which are conventional? Or is it a matter of the difference between the nature of the effects produced? Or might it be that our eccentric man's response is overwhelming whereas the response here is not?)

Most cases are not so straightforward. The presence in a work of a 'technical' feature known to commonly produce a certain response is not usually sufficient to ensure that response. Other features can influence its effect more or less strongly; for example, if the lines with the 'l' and 'r' sounds had been expressing something harsh and unpleasant, this might well lessen or even nullify the effect of fluency. In this way a particular case may be so intricate, and the feature in question so hedged about with other factors (as with Ricks' claim about the abba rhyme scheme) that it is impossible for us to judge whether it has its effect, even if it characteristically does have that effect. One of the difficulties in such cases is to separate the 'technical' feature from the sense — to know whether the sense is going counter to the effect of the feature, whether the one is reinforcing the other, or whether even the sense is producing the effect and not the feature at all. And indeed if they were easily separable, and if the connection between feature and effect were as reliable as we may seem to have been suggesting in earlier examples, poetry — and indeed criticism — would be a lesser art than it is. A good critic will be less interested in the gross effects which depend on obvious connections, than in those finer and more subtle effects which undoubtedly exist. The irony is that as his acuity is heightened so the possibility of testing what he says diminishes; and as it diminishes so the possibility that acuity will be replaced by over-reading and invention, indeed by self-indulgence, by a parasitic second-class creativity, grows.

The matters we have been discussing make it easy to see why so often the word 'normal' has a double force; it is both descriptive and normative. But the inference that wherever a reaction is not normal it is therefore wrong is itself wrong. We can envisage the possibility of a poet whose feeling of rhythm is hyper-acute, and of such a sort that his work will only appeal to, be 'understood' by, readers who share that acuity. (Hopkins is such a poet; and perhaps his feelings for rhythm were so acute that no-one has been able to share them fully). We can understand that such acuity might be a matter of envy amongst other persons who while able intellectually to recognise and identify this dimension in his work cannot respond to it.

But cases of this sort are not easily distinguished from others, which we should want to describe as involving not hyper-acuity but preciousness and over-sensitivity. Henry James' later style may raise such a problem, as indeed may Hopkins' rhythm. And cases of that sort have to be distinguished again from those where what is at issue is not the rightness of the hyper-sensitive response so much as the existence of that to which it is a response.

We have been talking about sensibility in connection with technical matters; and a question of sensibility is raised by yet another part of Ricks' criticism, but it involves matters of a very different sort. We are concerned here with Ricks' guarded claims that there is a 'subterranean idea' in the poem that 'the speaker is standing not just before Hallam's house but before Hallam's dead body', and that this is 'responsible for a great deal of the quiet force of the lines'. Now the existence of the idea in the poem, as Ricks himself admits, is problematic; establishing that it is there will consist in establishing that 'dark house' somehow alludes to Hallam's body, an allusion the reader has to recognise if he is to be aware of the idea. Ricks, taking more care in presenting a claim of which he is less certain, offers various arguments in support of its existence. He reminds — or perhaps informs — us that there is an ancient tradition, especially in funeral elegy, which sees the body as a sort of house, so there is a traditional precedent for this symbolic connection in poetry; and that indeed the Anglo-Saxon word for body was 'banhus'. Resisting possible accusations that these traditional associations are pagan, he points out that the idea is perfectly appropriate to Christian beliefs about the freedom of the soul when the body dies. Then using evidence of a rather different sort he points out that Tennyson had in fact made use of the idea explicitly in a poem written three years previously (a poem with a stanza form very like that of *In Memoriam*, and actually containing the phrase 'dark deserted house'). Finally, returning to this section of *In Memoriam* he suggests that if the symbolic idea were there this would provide a very satisfactory explanation of why Tennyson addresses the house.

But it is not at all clear that the imperative 'Behold me' is addressed to the house, it might be to the reader (or, of course, to both). Even if it is addressed to the house, this is not so extraordinary as to require some further explanation. And while the evidence for the claim that the house is addressed is ambiguous, there is something else in these first lines which actively works against Ricks' larger claim. For Tennyson refers to Hallam's hand, and the incongruity of his standing before Hallam's body 'waiting for a hand' can strike us as both ludicrous and obscene; though Ricks might reply here that just because the suggestion that the house is Hallam's body is not blatant, this incongruity will not be apparent.

The evidence of Tennyson's earlier poem is certainly relevant, (in spite of what New Critics might be tempted to argue) though not very strong or indeed unequivocal. As for the argument from tradition, this doesn't show that we immediately and pervasively connect 'dark house' with the idea of a dead body (in the way that we perhaps do connect 'dark' with connotations of gloom or death). In order for the reader to make that connection a more particular context is required (and we may have it here because of the subject matter), as is knowledge of a scholarly sort.[19]

So we have been presented with all the evidence relevant to the question of whether the 'subterranean idea' is present; but the conclusion is still doubtful — we are inclined to say, 'It may be there, but it may not be.' Now what does it mean to say this? It means that once we have this information, some of us find that 'dark house' does suggest Hallam's body, while others of us remain unconvinced. The idea to be resisted here is that it means that somehow the allusion is there and some of us perceive it and some of us do not; or conversely that it is not there, and some of us think it is there and other perceive that it is not.

But how do we arrive at our critical view? In a completely informal and intuitive way — how else might we proceed? One factor we haven't mentioned so far which may help us to come to a decision, is that most of us would feel it was a better poem if the subterranean idea *were* there. And since better poems are rarely achieved accidentally, independently of what the author is trying to do, this is a consideration which counts in favour of the view that the idea was intended — provided one agrees with Ricks that the poem is a good one.

At any rate, it is clear that differing views are possible, and they reflect differing judgements, differing sensibilities. What determines our view, as this discussion has shown, is an enormous variety of what seem to be imponderable and indeed incommensurable factors which nonetheless we somehow weigh. So the very existence of this idea in the poem involves judgement and sensibility, and this couldn't contrast more strongly with the existence of the abba rhyme scheme.[20]

But once this question is settled — supposing the existence of the 'subterranean idea' in the poem to be as unproblematic as that of the rhyme scheme — do we use our judgement in the same way in deciding what effect it does, and should have? And is a doubt about the claimed effect of the rhyme scheme of the same order as a doubt about the claimed effect of the subterranean idea?

The claim that the rhyme scheme has an effect appears to be, and may be construed as, an empirical, causal one, in which case the claim is that the rhyming words which in fact exhibit the abba pattern work on us as we read the poem, reinforcing the ebbing and flowing of feeling. But does the rhyme scheme really do this? We can not perceive this effect, and we do not even have the phenomenological experience of perceiving, or rather thinking that we perceive, the effect. The claim also depends on a bit of speculative psychology (that a distant rhyme creates only a distant, remote hope), and finally it is backed up by pointing to the congruity between the formal representation of the rhyme scheme and the (alleged) ebbing and flowing of feeling, and seeing this congruity can in turn have an effect on our response to the rhyme scheme.

But a man can doubt that the rhyme scheme does tend to reinforce the ebb and flow of feeling in the poem, though experiment is not possible here. Moreover it could affect him and yet he might not be aware of this and could coherently doubt that it does so. So he could certainly doubt that it ought to do so; for to say this is to say little more than that it has the alleged effect for most readers. Even if he conceded that, he might still feel that this response is somehow not required of him, at least not in the case of this particular poem, perhaps because of the interference of other factors.

But at any rate the judgement that this technical feature has an effect and ought to have an effect involves our sensibility primarily in this way: we are required to make a speculative intuitive judgement about what would appear to be an elusive matter of fact.

Now compare this with the question, 'Does the subterranean idea give the lines a force that they would otherwise lack?' Certainly it gives them a dimension they would otherwise lack. Moreover in this case there seems little possibility that one could be affected by the subterranean idea without being aware of it, as one could be affected by the rhyme scheme without being aware of it. At least, in order for this possibility to be realised one would have to imagine that the man was suppressing his awareness of the subterranean idea, whereas in contrast the person who is affected by the rhyme scheme without being aware of it, in the sense that he hadn't realised it was in the abba form — and might even be unable to say this on reflection — is not, or at any rate need not be, suppressing knowledge. Similarly, the suggestion that we might be aware of the subterranean idea and affected by it, and yet not aware that we are affected by it, seems to make little sense whereas a similar suggestion in connection with the rhyme scheme makes perfectly good sense.[21] For again, the only way we can make sense of the suggestion that we are affected by the subterranean idea but not aware that we are affected by it or how we are affected by it, is to think that we suppress or repress this awareness. We mention the possibility of suppression and repression here, not merely to cover ourselves against a bare possibility, but because it may very well be the case that poetry — and particularly modern poetry — gets much of its effect by touching on deep feelings of whose existence and nature we are not fully aware.

Why is it, then, that we cannot have a direct awareness of the effect of the rhyme scheme, whereas we can have such knowledge of the effect of the subterranean idea? The hypothetical contribution made by the rhyme scheme, which after all is an auxiliary one, is a brute one — although we strive to reinforce the plausibility of the claim that it exists by considerations of a 'rational' kind, which considerations themselves have a non-rational consequence both for our view here and indeed our response to the rhyme scheme. Establishing its existence then is rather like establishing, say, that it is alcohol which makes you feel dizzy, or that it is the beer which you have recently drunk which is making you feel dizzy now; and our moral certainty on matter of this sort really does depend on establishing brute connections, not on perceiving them.

We can draw an analogy between the effect, or the alleged effect, of the abba rhyme scheme in this section of *In Memoriam*, and the effect which nitrous oxide has when it is inhaled. Nitrous oxide makes people laugh, but that it makes people laugh is an effect which the subjects do not and indeed cannot perceive, and which has to be established by experiment.[22] Now compare laughter of this sort with our laughing at a joke or at a comedy, our being amused. Here we are not simply being made to laugh by something, we are laughing at it. The joke or whatever is, as Wittgenstein would have said, not (just) the cause of our laughter but its object or target. We do not have to perform experiments in order to determine what we are laughing at; indeed we cannot perform experiments to test whether what a man sincerely says he is laughing at is what he is laughing at.

Now to say that the joke, or whatever, is the target of a man's amusement is not to deny, as some have though,[23] that it is its cause. Indeed, if a man is in such a condition that he would laugh at whatever one said to him, the joke one uttered and which 'makes' him laugh is only the target of his laughter and not its cause. So that if we describe a play as funny we are not merely saying that it will be the object of an audience's amusement, but that it will be the cause of their amusement.[24]

Just as a response to this rhyme scheme corresponds to a reaction to nitrous oxide, so, we suggest, a response to the subterranean idea is of the same sort as a response to the joke. If we are affected by the idea that the dark house is also in some way Hallam's dead body — and responses differ according to differing sensibilities here — our response is directed towards that idea. And even if, being aware of the idea, a man fails to respond, or responds bizarrely, his failure to respond is a response to the idea even though a negative one; it is directed towards the idea, and in articulating it he has to refer to the idea: 'I am not moved by this idea'. So the subterranean idea is the target of one's response. This doesn't circumscribe the content of the response, how a man responds, but only its direction.

So what we have argued here is that, if a man is aware of the subterranean idea and is affected by it, that he is affected and how he is affected are not matters about which he might speculate or be mistaken.[25] Nor are they things we would need to test by experiment. (Yet just because the subterranean idea is not a formal feature or a matter of literal meaning or pervasive connotations, it would be possible for a man to read the poem and not be aware of it at all, in contrast with the rhyme scheme where on some level and in some way he must be aware of it. So, ironically, we can perform an experiment to test what contribution if any, is made by this idea, namely by persuading readers who had been unaware of it that it is there in the poem and then asking them, 'Now how does this strike you?')

What then can be at issue here when we ask, 'Is the subterranean idea responsible (in part) for the quiet force of the lines?' We are not asking whether the subterranean idea is the cause of a man's response, or at least we would not think arguments about that to be relevant. That it is the target doesn't, of course, mean that it is the cause, but there is no reason for thinking here that it is not. For the idea of a man's addressing the dead body of a friend is the sort of thing that might well in fact impress one. So what we are really asking here is what contribution the subterranean idea *ought* to make, how it ought to affect one.

Now what kind of question is this? In arguing about this a man might defend his failure to respond on the grounds that this idea, though it is an inherently powerful one — and it is of this very notion, of its being inherently powerful, that we must give an account — is spoilt by other features in the poem, perhaps by the poor quality of the rest of the poem, and this is an aesthetic objection. Or again he might say that it is spoilt not by the rest of the poem but by the idea's not being sufficiently *there*, not sufficiently realised — again, an aesthetic objection. Both objections involve one's sensibility. But suppose he does not mention either of these things; we are left with the claim that a poet's addressing the dead body of his friend is not profound or moving. But, if his reason for saying that is not, again, that it has become hackneyed, or something of that sort, what we are left with is a claim that most of us would find very curious, not about what men in fact find moving, but rather about what ought to move them. Here the issue becomes a sort of moral one, an argument about how men ought to feel. (Of course, a man, in saying that he does not find the idea moving, may intend no more than what he says, *viz.*, that *he* is not moved by the idea. But unless he is prepared to admit that his sensibility is defective here, most of us will construe his bald, apparently 'factual' assertion that he does not find the idea moving — 'I'm not claiming any more than that' — as indicating, not that he is wrong about the nature of his feelings, but that most of us are wrong, and as challenging the claim that he ought to feel moved.)

What is at issue finally, then, is not an epistemological matter, but a species of moral one. In asking, 'Does the subterranean idea make any contribution to the "quiet force" of the lines?', we are not speculating about whether the idea does in fact have a certain effect but whether our moral sensibility is involved here.

Now of course it is always open to a man charged with moral insensitivity in connection with his response to works of art to distinguish the 'fact', as it were — in this case a man's addressing the body of his dead friend — from mere allusions to such facts, particularly as these allusions occur in works of art. The former is aweful, that is, indeed powerful or moving, and he is properly awed by it, but a so-called 'failure' to respond to the latter has no moral implications at all. Why should he respond to Tennyson's literary device? And how absurd to infer that he is unfeeling about death and friendship if he does not.

The distinction is genuine, and the defence against even a species of moral criticism is itself very powerful. Nonetheless, literary devices such as Tennyson's must ultimately get their power to move us from the facts to which they allude, and if their failure to move a man is not explained away aesthetically, a species of moral criticism remains. 'Ask not for whom the bell tolls: it tolls for thee': the man who insists on the aesthetic objection here will surely be felt to be an aesthete in that strong sense which makes it a moral criticism. And if there is a double difficulty in proving such a charge, namely that moral assertions cannot themselves be strictly proved, and in any case the charge can always be turned aside by pleading an aesthetic objection, it will still be felt and made.

The man who employs the 'aesthetic' defence in this example — the man who finds the fact of a man's addressing the body of his dead friend moving, but not this veiled allusion to it— may have a strong case. After all, all we have in the poem is the mention of 'dark house' and, if we accept Ricks' thesis, an allusion through that phrase to Hallam's body. But now if we look at Ricks criticism we will see that although his remarks about, in particular, 'banhus' are presented as if they were merely intended to support the claim that the subterranean idea is there in the poem, their effect is greater than this; their tendency, at any rate, is to inflate the subterranean idea, and in a marvellous way. We could almost be persuaded when we read Ricks that Tennyson himself in using the phrase 'dark house' has alluded not merely to Hallam's body but to his body as a 'banhus'.

For the mention of 'banhus' transforms the simple idea of Tennyson standing before the house which is also his friends dead body, into one which is rich in associations which reverberate. What a world of difference there is between 'dark house' and 'banhus'. 'Banhus' provides the magical link between the ordinary words 'house' and 'body'. In describing the body as a 'house of bones' it reminds us that our bodies only clothe our skeletons for a brief time; we feel 'the skull beneath the flesh', the body encompassing its own mortality, and yet, ironically, supported by it — a structure which is echoed in the actual construction of many Anglo-Saxon houses, timber frames fleshed in clay. So that even by the element 'house' we are thrown back to the idea of our own mortality. The ideas contained in 'banhus' infect both 'house' and 'body'; the subterranean idea, if it is there in Tennyson's poem, does suddenly seem a rich and powerful one.

So when we read 'house' in the poem we may feel the richness of these associations, though we will be uncertain of whether Tennyson intended them or not; or on the other hand we may find the idea in the poem disappointingly thin in comparison with Ricks' account of it, and so we may feel it to be a feature which is there but which has failed. Ricks seems guilty not only of over-ingenuity here, but of over-ingenuity which may actually weaken the poem he strives to praise.

The weight then lies again on the question of whether the subterranean idea is there (in the sense of being there and sufficiently realised). But if this question is settled, if the idea is there in that full sense, certainly we feel it to be an idea which should move and disturb, just as the fact to which it refers should move and disturb; and if it does not we will think the reader's response, and his sensibility, defective, and not just aesthetically but morally. No such claims could be made about a failure to respond to the rhyme scheme.

We have so minutely anatomised what Ricks has to say — and have still ignored the bulk of it — that a reader might understandably object that the enquiry is absurd, it is too detailed.

But we have been seeking to show, both by this close examination, and by the many discussions in the previous two chapters, that critical arguments are frequently complex, elusive and rhetorically misleading as to their true nature, very diverse, and often dubious. The minuteness is necessary to that demonstration, just as the demonstration truly is necessary, even to those who feel that they are already aware that criticism is like this. Certainly, if critics profess to such awareness there is an incongruity between that and the confidence with which they write. It is our belief that enquiries such as this can help critics, and others, towards a clearer understanding of the problems involved in practising criticism, and of the consequences for its practice.

4 Are there any necessary conditions of excellence in art?

In our section on Leavis and Fogle we considered the questions: is 'particularity' a *desideratum* in poetry, and if it is, how could this be shewn? Fogle seemed to think that Leavis was committed to the claim that it (always) is a *desideratum*, and objected that such a critical position is too narrow. Leavis on the other hand, seemed to feel that what the good critic values cannot helpfully — or cannot *tout court* — be specified in any general way (and so he isn't committed to a general claim. What he has to say can only be fully understood in relation to the work he is criticising. But even if Leavis is right about this, it still leaves us with the question of the correctness of, and basis for, his particular evaluations).

However, this disagreement, with others we have examined, raises two large questions which we shall try to answer in our concluding chapters. The first could be put this way: are there any quite general criteria of excellence in art, or are there criteria within some spheres of art, such as poetry perhaps, and can this be shewn? The second, which we examine in our next, concluding chapter is: if the quest for canons of aesthetic excellence seems fruitless, may this not be because, as some think, critical reasons are logically singular and cannot be generalised? Or must critical reasons, being reasons, be general?

In this chapter we shall be concerned primarily with whether there are any necessary conditions of excellence in art. Clearly the enormous variety of art means that if there are pervasively applicable conditions of excellence, these qualities are of such abstraction that they will scarcely be mentioned by critics engaged in criticism; and for that reason, if no other, critics may be sceptical about their existence. But the belief that there are more local necessary conditions has engaged critics. For example, Johnson's appreciation of Shakespeare's plays led him to ask if the unities were necessary conditions of excellence in drama, and we begin this chapter by looking at his discussion.

To the unities of time and place he   [Shakespeare] has shown no regard: and perhaps a nearer view of the principles on which they stand will diminish their value and withdraw from them the veneration which, from the time of Corneille, they have very generally received, by discovering that they have given more trouble to the poet than pleasure to the auditor.

The necessity of observing the unities of time and place arises from the supposed necessity of making the drama credible. The critics hold it impossible that an action of months or years can be possibly believed to pass in three hours; or that the spectator can suppose himself to sit in the theatre while ambassadors go and return between distant kings, while armies are levied and towns besieged, while an exile wanders and returns, or till he whom they saw courting his mistress shall lament the untimely fall of his son. The mind revolts from evident falsehood, and fiction loses its force when it departs from the resemblance of reality.

From the narrow limitation of time necessarily arises the contraction of place. The spectator, who knows that he saw the first act at Alexandria, cannot suppose that he sees the next at Rome, at a distance to which not the dragons of Medea could, in so short a time, have transported him; he knows with certainty that he has not changed his place; and he knows that place cannot change itself; that what was a house cannot become a plain; that what was Thebes can never be Persepolis.

Such is the triumphant language with which a critic exults over the misery of an irregular poet and exults commonly without resistance or reply. It is time, therefore, to tell him by the authority of Shakespeare, that he assume, as an unquestionable principle, a position which, while his breath is forming it into words, his understanding pronounces to be false. It is false, that any representation is mistaken for reality; that any dramatic fable in its materiality was ever credible, or, for a single moment, was ever credited.

The objection arising from the impossibility of passing the first hour at Alexandria and the next at Rome, supposes that when the play opens the spectator really imagines himself at Alexandria and believes that his walk to the theatre has been a voyage to Egypt, and that he lives in the days of Anthony and Cleopatra. Surely he that imagines this may imagine more. He that can take the stage at one time for the palace of the Ptolemies may take it in half an hour for the promontory of Actium. Delusion, if delusion be admitted, has no certain limitation; if the spectator can be once more persuaded that his old acquaintance are Alexander and Caesar, that a room illuminated with candles is the plain of Pharsalia or the bank of Granicus, he is in a state of elevation above the reach of reason or of truth, and from the heights of empyrean poetry may despise the circumscriptions of terrestrial nature. There is no reason why a mind thus wandering in ecstasy should count the clock, or why an hour should not be a century in that calenture of the brains that can make the stage a field.

The truth is that the spectators are always in their senses and know, from the first act to the last that the stage is only a stage, and that the players are only players. They come to hear a certain number of lines recited with just gesture and elegant modulation. The lines relate to some action, and an action must be in some place; but the different actions that complete a story may be in places very remote from each other; and where is the absurdity of allowing that space to represent first Athens and then Sicily, which was always known to be neither Sicily nor Athens, but a modern theatre.

By supposition, as place is introduced, time may be extended; the time required by the fable elapses for the most part between the acts; for, of so much of the action as is represented, the real and poetical duration is the same. If in the first act preparations for war against Mithridates are represented to be made in Rome, the event of the war may, without absurdity, be represented in the catastrophe as happening in Pontus; we know that there is neither war nor preparation for war; we know that we are neither in Rome nor Pontus; that neither Mithridates nor Lucullus are before us. The drama exhibits successive imitations of successive actions; and why may not the second imitation represent an action that happened years after the first, if it be so connected with it that nothing but time can be supposed to intervene? Time is, of all modes of existence, most obsequious to the imagination; a lapse of years is as easily conceived as a passage of hours. In contemplation we easily contract the time of real actions and therefore willingly permit it to be contracted when we only see their imitation.

Preface to Shakespeare, Vol. VII pp. 75–8.

Aristotle's sometimes tentative and cryptic remarks in the *Poetics* concerning the so-called 'unities' of action and time were extended and strengthened by Renaissance critics into a doctrine, *viz*. that plays must exhibit the unities of action, time and, often, place, if they were to be good and unflawed.

A traditional justification of the unities of time and place, which are the two whose status Johnson attacks, is that unless a play is unified in these ways it will lack credibility. But, if this is true, it would seem to be contingently true, and that it is false might be thought to be demonstrable by means of counter-examples, i.e., plays which, though they depict events taking place at times separated by more than 24 hours, or in different locales, are nonetheless 'credible'; which here means that they engage their audiences and the change of time and place do not shatter their audiences' 'suspension of disbelief'.

Johnson's attack is not so direct, or simple, as this. He attempts instead a species of *reductio*, pointing out that if an audience cannot accept the rapid change of scene from Alexandria to Rome, it equally cannot accept that it is in the first place witnessing in London an action which takes place at Alexandria. Johnson has here scored a palpable hit, and initially we may be inclined to think that he has succeeded in showing that this defence (from credibility) of these unities is incoherent. Had Johnson done so it would not be possible for a conservatively minded critic to assert what may in fact be the case *viz*., that *he* finds that such plays lack credibility, or whether he does or not that audiences *ought* not to find these plays credible.

What Johnson has done is to point out that an audience's accepting that successive acts take place at widely separated locations involves no fresh principle that is not involved in their accepting that the action of some entire play occurs in some locale remote from their own. Nonetheless, audiences might find that whilst the first leap of imagination is possible, successive leaps are more difficult. And precisely this constitutes and forms a part of the conservative critic's instrumental justification of the unities of time and place.

Construed as an *a priori* refutation of the defence from credibility, Johnson's argument fails, but its apparent power is not wholly illusory. For Johnson shows us, or, rather, he states, and we recognise the truth of his statement, that despite what traditional critics may have said audiences can find plays which lack the unities of time and place credible, for they do so! The instrumental justification is in fact mistaken, and its refutation depends not on revealing a howler but on making an observation in spite of the blinkering critical theory.

But as Johnson recognises, there may be other and possibly better defences of the unities of time and place.[1] But what are these? A conservatively minded critic might concede, as was mentioned before, that plays lacking the unities may be found credible by audiences, yet insist that to respond in this way is to be guilty of some error of sensibility, but why is this? It is not part of our very concept of a play that its action should take place in one spot and be completed within a day; and even if it were[2] it would not follow that works of art that were not strictly speaking plays were therefore inferior to true plays and did not merit our aesthetic responses to them.

One suspects that the traditional critic may feel, and might argue, not that the plays whose merit is in question lack credibility, or should do, but that to find them credible, engaging, or really good plays is vulgar. For such plays give too much liberty to the writer and lack a tightness of structure and an economy of means which are aesthetically fine, and this is what should be pleasing.

This argument has some merit; Johnson himself decries, for example, the value of spectacle whilst recognising its appeal. But is it true that a play must be easier to write if these unities are not observed? If they are not observed, the playwright may have to tackle problems which cannot otherwise arise, for example that of showing the process of ageing. And is it true that such plays must lack a felt unity? There are no doubt examples of such plays which will be felt to sprawl, but the thesis at issue is that such plays must sprawl.

It is the arguments we have devised for the traditional critic which lack credibility, not the plays he would condemn, and though to say this is not to refute his position, is refutation of such a critical thesis possible — except where it is internally inconsistent?

A possible explanation of why some critics continued to insist on the unities of time and place after Shakespeare had written his plays is that what originally could be justified on the grounds that compliance with them made for credibility later came to acquire a prestige beyond and in addition to that merited by their serving this purpose. So that when they were found to be unnecessary for this purpose they were still felt to be right and some further justification had to be found for them. Moreover, the feeling that the unities must be observed, and the belief that they were necessary for credibility could themselves produce in critics responses to new works which in a self-verifying fashion confirmed their critical theories. What start as practical maxims ('Do not put saturated colours side by side, it is displeasing') can become self-supporting critical principles.[3]

If the preceding remarks are correct, the unities of time and place are not really desirable in themselves, although they tend to acquire an intrinsic desirability for some, but are only desirable if and when they help to produce a certain end, in this case credibility.

This invites the question: is then credibility itself a *sine qua non* of excellence in drama? Now we can easily think of works which if they lacked credibility would not be as good as they are, but if Bertolt Brecht's work does not strive for credibility, and does not achieve it, can we say that, therefore, his plays are flawed, lesser works or that they would be better if they did not 'alienate' their audiences?

It is precisely this problem of which Johnson is aware in his discussion of the unities of time and place. He concedes the thesis that they may have some value, but it is the insistence that they are necessary conditions of good drama which he resists, particularly as he suspects that whatever original justification they may have had has been forgotten, and only the principle remains. No-one argues better than Johnson against mechanical adherence to a critical principle.[4]

Yet with regard to the unity of action, Johnson largely agrees with Aristotle. Unless a play depicts an 'action', roughly, an episode of some magnitude and importance in the life of a man, which is complete in itself, a play will lack a beginning, middle or end. (To put the point informally, part of the plot will be missing.) Conversely, if a play encompasses more than one such action, it will lack unity and really be two or more plays. Unity of action then is a necessary condition of a play's being unflawed.

Is this view correct, and if it is not why does Johnson accept it? It is of course true that there are plays which strike us as not being wholly satisfactory because some part of the story they tell is missing, and there are others which don't seem to hang together but are composed of two or more unrelated themes. Their unsatisfactoriness could be explained in terms of, and constituted by their action being incomplete or not forming a single whole.

But are there not also plays which do not present us with the complete episode with which they deal, and yet are not felt to lack unity? Are there not others which clearly involve episodes perhaps in the lives of two different persons, which do not physically overlap or interact, yet which yield an integrated aesthetic whole?

It may be objected that despite formal appearances to the contrary such plays do not really lack unity of action, because their plots do not strike us as incomplete or fragmented, and it is no doubt true that in many cases we could say whether the 'action' of a play was unified or not except through and in terms of our responses to it. 'Unity of action' may stand for (as perhaps 'unity of time' and 'unity of place' could not) the *impression* a play gives us of being a unified whole. (This may explain why Johnson accepts it as a necessary condition and explains why we discuss it.) In such cases, 'unity of action' would almost be a term of praise and we would perhaps never use it to describe the defects of a play.

Even so, are there not works which do not even strike us as complete, in which perhaps we are left hanging in the air, and where that lack of dénouement might strike us as absolutely right? Conversely, can we say in advance that a play might not present a collection of unrelated themes, themes which do not strike us as related, and yet impress us as a good, even a great, play — perhaps precisely because we find in it a lack of unity and multiplicity of themes which is like life itself? And how could it possibly be shown or even claimed that our feelings about these plays, *viz.* that they were good not despite their lack of unity of action but precisely because of it, *must* be wrong?

The belief that there are necessary conditions of excellence in drama, i.e. that every play must exemplify certain characteristics if it is to be a good play, is now perhaps beginning to look a little implausible. But is this surprising? Plays after all differ so much from each other that what will be appropriate and even necessary for the success of one might be quite out of place in another. Whatever the beliefs and intellectual ambitions of aestheticians, most critics, particularly practical critics, are aware that they do not criticise works in general but particular works. Few of them would think it possible to say in advance that a play he is about to see must possess certain features if it is to be good.

But although this is true, and may explain a practical critic's impatience with aesthetics, it does not follow that the aesthetician who believes that there are and indeed must be necessary conditions, or at least some sort of criteria of excellence in drama is wrong. Plays differ amongst themselves, but it does not follow that it is not the case that at some level good plays all have something in common in virtue of which they are good, just as it is natural to assume plays themselves all have something in common in virtue of which they are plays. The impossibility of being able to say in advance what traits a good play must exemplify may merely reflect the fact that the level of the critic's discussion is particular, and he will find different things to commend in different works, but his use of critical terms may presuppose a more abstract, higher order set of criteria which are not only general but necessary.

If this is felt to be mere intellectual speculation, the philosopher of criticism has another point in favour of a related though weaker thesis which he may see as *a priori* true. It is that although of course the critic's discussion of works is particular, if in his criticism he offers *reasons* for thinking a work good those reasons, being reasons, *must be general*.

We shall return to these points. But another source of doubt about the existence of necessary conditions which appeared in our earlier discussion is not answered even if the philosopher's thesis about reasons is correct. It is that though perhaps different individuals have their own sets of criteria of excellence for works of art, which may or may not function as necessary conditions in their criticism, these values differ to a lesser or greater extent from critic to critic. Of course it does not follow that some values are not right and others wrong, but if in the case of those values where critics disagree, one set could be shown to be right and others wrong, why has disagreement not been ended by a demonstration? If demonstration is not possible, what does it mean to say that a certain critical criterion of excellence in art, though right, cannot be shown to be right?

But again it has to be said that these points, though well taken, do not justify scepticism about the existence of neces-

sary conditions in criticism. Critics do differ, but not totally.
And it does not follow that because some individuals have not
been satisfied that some thesis or other is true, that it is not
true, and has not been proved to be true.

Returning then to our pursuit of necessary conditions of excellence in drama, our quest might be more successful if we
looked for what might be called 'local' necessary conditions,
i.e. necessary conditions of excellence within different species
of the genus drama; and what could be clearer or more obvious than that funniness is a necessary condition of a (modern)
comedy's being a good one?[5] That a comedy should be funny is
a requirement which a critic certainly can state in advance, and
when he gives this reason (perhaps amongst others) for thinking a particular comedy a good one he will be using a criterion
which he not only applies to all comedies but one whose use he
is able to justify — if justification were ever wanted. To say
that a comedy should be funny is the flattest of tautologies.

   Despite this there are disagreements concerning the merits
of particular comedies because persons disagree as to whether
they are funny. Some of Joe Orton's comedies, e.g. *Entertaining Mr. Sloane*, attracted disagreement of this sort. Of course,
disagreements also exist over the application of other critical
terms. But, as we noticed earlier, although 'funny' is used of
the work or part of the work and 'funniness' designates a
property of the work or part of the work, the existence and
identification of that which is funny depends on our response.
Something is funny if it strikes us as being funny. In this way,
being funny, unlike the unities of time and place, is not what
might be called a formal quality. So its application as a criterion could not help to resolve disagreements about comedies
which already exist. And since it is a tautological criterion,
saying that funniness is a necessary condition does not help to
lay bare the structure of our critical thinking about comedies.

Part of the *raison d'etre* of the search for necessary conditions
of excellence in art is to find a foundation for critical evaluations. But the discovery of local necessary conditions can still
leave us with that problem. For it does not follow that if a

work meets a requirement for being a good comedy, or melodrama, it therefore meets a requirement for being a good play.[6] (The contrary, indeed, may follow with melodrama.) Similar problems occur in poetry; good clerihews are not, therefore, good poems, and indeed for some critics it would seem that a necessary condition of a poem's being a good Augustan poem is a sufficient condition of its being a less good poem.[7] Such general terms as 'pastiche' present a similar problem.

We are searching for criteria of aesthetic excellence and it is more likely to occur to a philosopher than a critic that just as it does not, or may not, follow from something's being a good member of some species of artistic genus that it is a good member of that genus, it may not necessarily follow from its being a good member of that genus that it is a good work of art. In fact, doubts about the aesthetic merits of members of an entire genus of works have been felt by critics. Film, for example, was not considered to be a serious form of art in its earlier years, as the lack of serious film criticism in that period bears witness. But do we need a proof that a good play is therefore a good work of art, and, if we do, what better proof could we have than the existence of such plays as *Hamlet*?

If we are looking for necessary conditions of aesthetic excellence, especially in drama, it might be suggested that we look at the necessary conditions of a good tragedy, the reason being that the inferences from a play's being a good tragedy to its being a good play and indeed a good work of art don't seem problematic, as we've just noticed. Although this is so, unless we assume that only tragedies are good or possibly the best plays and the best dramatic works of art, those conditions which are necessary for a play's being a good tragedy won't be necessary for a play's being a good play or a good work of art, but only sufficient for that.[7]

Another point which arises from this discussion is that we might want to distinguish between a condition which is necessary for a play's being a good play and other conditions which are necessary for a play's being excellent, i.e. for being the best sort of play. A critic may wish to say that certainly comedies can be good plays, and if our discussion suggests the contrary, this is wrong; it's rather that comedies perhaps can't be the best or the greatest plays. This is a point worth making, but the possibility of making it depends on the fact that we've been trying to discuss the necessary conditions for the application of a phrase which includes a term that has a comparative and a superlative; so this kind of ambiguity is very difficult to avoid.

But we are presently in pursuit of necessary conditions of excellence, if only in drama, and to hope to find them by looking for necessary conditions of excellence of a certain species of this artistic genus is already to give up the pursuit, unless we then go on to ask what the connection is between the conditions sufficient for a play's being a good tragedy, and those necessary for a play's being a good play — which is to return us to our original question. Apart from the difficulty that this sort of species criticism can become artificial and lead us to ignore the existence of plays which cannot be categorised, or into ludicrous attempts to categorise them ('pastoral-comical, historical-pastoral, tragical-historical, tragical-comical-historical-pastoral'), doing this can blind us to the possibility that good plays *do* have features in common in virtue of which they are good, and at a fairly concrete level.

But even if we were able to discover these features common to good plays, if indeed they exist, we should still be left with the question of the connection between these and, what the aesthetician wants and believes to exist, namely, criteria of aesthetic excellence which are common to all the arts. What we now propose to do is to examine a couple of plausible candidates for this status and then look at some suggested by aestheticians.

Skill has obvious appeal as a criterion: it is generally applicable, its desirability as a criterion doesn't seem to require argument, and it is widely accepted. However, it must be immediately conceded that skill in a work is a necessary condition if it is one at all, only in the weak sense that its absence is a defect, but not a disabling one; a work can be good or great in spite of that.

But is not even this weak claim too strong? For there are some works which are good not just despite their lack of skill but because of it. Primitive painters characteristically lack certain basic skills of craftsmanship, they work superbly indifferent to the development of art, and the training which is available to artists. So that their work is naive and being invariably representational can be seen, in comparison with that of even the most ordinary of professional painters, to be unskilful.[8] Yet their lack of skill is constitutive of their appeal and not just in the weak sense that it makes some other virtue possible, but in the stronger sense that it contributes crucially to the impression of innocence and of being given an insight into a highly personal vision.[9]

But the sense of freshness, which the comparative ineptitude of the primitives produces, is parasitic on the centrality of skill and our sensitivity to it in the main tradition of art. Their clumsiness and attendant *naiveté* would surely not delight if it were the rule rather than the exception; imagine all our galleries full of such paintings. Perhaps because we realise this we do not judge these paintings by the same standards as we apply to most works of art.[10]

If we had to characterise skill in the aesthetician's terms, we would be more inclined to call it a 'good-making feature' or a virtue rather than a necessary condition whilst recognising that there are works which if *per impossibile* they were skilful would lose their other virtues. Yet within this latter group there is a sub-group the existence of whose virtues is parasitic on skill's being a virtue. In this weakened way skill survives as a criterion of excellence.

That it survives as a criterion of excellence shouldn't surprise us, because often to say that a work is skilful is, very roughly, to say that it is done well. But 'skill' is then too closely related to our notion of excellence to give any analysis of it.

However to say that a work that is done well is a good work, is too strong, and, as we have seen, works which are not done well are not always, therefore, less good than they would be if *per impossibile* they were done well. We do not have here a tautology like 'A good man is one who acts well'.

Some artists have felt that all that a critic can properly demand is that an artist be skilful, that is, do whatever he chooses to do well. We may criticise his 'execution' or 'realisation', but not what Henry James called his *donnée*.[11] But we can agree with James that the artist must be allowed his *donnée* yet still, and properly, evaluate his choice once it has been made. Of course an artist can also exhibit skill in what he chooses to do, but he can also exhibit qualities which cannot be reduced to skill, such as imagination and originality.

Shakespeare not original.

What then of originality? Before we go on to discuss this, we should notice one objection to construing either skill or originality as necessary conditions, made notably by Monroe Beardsley, that these are 'genetic' properties which are probably attributable not to the work but to the artist.[12] But although it is the artist who is skilful, his skill is realised in his work; the notion of skill brings together the artist and the work. Beardsley, as is well known, objects to any reference in the appreciation of art to the intention of the artist, and we have criticised this before. If 'skill' and 'originality' and many other terms we use in the appreciation of art are to be disallowed because they contain a reference to intention, isn't Beardsley reducing our appreciation of them, what we say about them, to the same level as our appreciation of 'works' of nature?[13]

Beardsley might defend himself against our criticism by saying that they tell only against a thesis cruder than his; that of course critical terms which include reference to intention are applicable, but properly applicable only to works where the intention is realised in the work (or sufficiently realised to make the intention evident). But in that case 'skill', 'skilful', etc., are legitimate critical terms. If Beardsley objects that the judgement that a work is skilful always involves an inference, and that that inference, whatever our moral certainty, is problematic (and not just irrelevant) the reduction in critical terminology and the parallel withering of our appreciation of art are dramatic. We shall not, for example, be able to speak of Jane Austen's wit, since however morally certain we are that she intends her humour it is logically possible that she does not and unless she does it is not wit, it is unconscious humour. Nor, of course, will we be able to call it that; in fact, we will lack a vocabulary in which to conduct a discussion.

The only thing which can be said for Beardsley's thesis is

that we have to distinguish between what a man intends to do and what he succeeds in doing; in art we have to judge the achievement. But what sense can we make of the notion of achievement itself if critical terms are not allowed any reference to intention?

'Originality' as it is used in criticism is a term which is used in various and sometimes idiosyncratic ways. For instance to say of Rembrandt's work, 'how original', would seem to diminish it, and perhaps the reason is that such remarks stress the novelty of the work in question rather than the quality of what is novel; though of course this does not mean that Rembrandt and similar artists are not in fact doing something novel. But whatever the variations in the way we use the term, and however immediate our judgements that a work is original, the notion of originality is ineluctably comparative.

Yet its being comparative does not mean that originality even in its weakest sense could not be a necessary condition of excellence; here novelty could be a *desideratum* even though it is a purely comparative feature, just as is speed in racehorses or strength in weightlifters. Indeed, originality in this weak sense seems to have become not just a virtue among contemporary artists but almost the only virtue left, and for fairly obvious reasons. But even amongst some contemporary artists, not just any novelty is thought to be good. In fact not just any substantial novelty is usually thought to be good or 'interesting', even though this might assure a work a place in the history of art — think, for example, of the anthropomorphic Victorian paintings of animals, notably those by Sir Edwin Landseer.

To judge that something is original and in so doing to commend it is to say not that it is simply novel in some respect, but that what is new about it is itself valuable, and is doubly valuable because it is new.

'Original', like 'skilful', then, is too close to being a tautological criterion of artistic excellence to interest aestheticians; as it involves that concept it can give no analysis of it. Yet it is not empty to say that originality is a *desideratum* in art, for to say this presupposes that something novel can have merit, and though this may strike contemporary western readers as no presupposition at all, some cultures have appeared to question this, to act indeed as if they believed the contrary, *viz.* that something new could not be good in art. In certain high cultures art is static, the artist's task is to produce traditional work. We see him as a folk artist or even as a mere craftsman, whose artistic virtue is simply his technical skill.

Aestheticians, however, are looking for more substantial criteria; criteria which at some level do specify the nature or the manner of the content, organisation, etc., of the work, and which are satisfied by particular features that can be found in every good work of art.

Clive Bell's 'significant form' has been construed as such a criterion, though there is an ambiguity in Bell's thinking which makes it unclear whether he thinks of it exactly as such; nor is it clear whether it applies to all the arts or only to the visual arts and perhaps music. 'Significant form' is worth examining if only because it has a great vogue amongst aestheticians and critics in the earlier part of this century, and it has been held that its discovery has led to developments in epistemology.[14]

Bell begins with the claim that works of art, or at any rate works of visual art,[15] must all have some common and peculiar quality, for unless this is so 'we gibber'. But since Wittgenstein's discussion of 'family resemblances'[16] and such articles as D. Gasking's 'Clusters'[17] the view that it is necessary if a term is to be meaningful that the things to which it applies must have something in common and peculiar to them cannot be assumed. Bell goes on to assert that 'All sensitive people agree that there is a peculiar emotion provoked by works of art', and this he calls the 'aesthetic emotion' (p. 17).

Aesthetic emotion is that provoked purely by the formal elements in a work, and not by any descriptive or narrative content it may have. (It is akin to the pleasure mathematicians find in elegant proofs.) He further asserts that the task of the aesthetician is to discover that quality which is common and peculiar to all works of art in virtue of which they provoke the aesthetic emotion.[18] What is this?

Only one answer seems possible — significant form. In 'all objects that provoke our aesthetic emotions' lines and colours combined in a particular way, certain forms and relations of forms, stir our aesthetic emotions.[19]

So good works of art (or as Bell would say, works which are indeed works of art) are distinguished by their capacity to provoke this emotion. This emotion then is defined partly in terms of its content and partly in terms of that at which it is directed. An emotional response to a work is not an aesthetic emotion unless it is non-humanistic and is directed at and provoked by the 'formal' elements of the work. So if someone's appreciation of a Rembrandt portrait was expressed in terms of its poignancy or honesty this wouldn't be an aesthetic response. However much he might value the painting in this way, it wouldn't have *aesthetic* value for him. This dimension of Bell's thinking is not vacuous[20] but controversial. For we need an argument to establish that such responses are not aesthetic ones and lack aesthetic value and that in some way they are irrelevant or even improper responses to something which is a work of art.

But suppose we accepted Bell's claims about the nature and value of aesthetic emotions; could Bell's discovery of significant form help us to resolve disagreements as to the aesthetic merits of different works? It couldn't, and to be fair to Bell he doesn't think that it could (hence the difficulty of construing it as a criterion). For, as he recognises, different persons are sensible to different works and no argument can demonstrate that something is a work of art to someone insensitive to it. Bell speaks vaguely of 'certain unknown and mysterious laws' (p. 19) which connect aesthetic emotion and 'forms arranged and combined' (p. 19), but he never actually seeks to establish them. And how could he if a work's having significant form depends on someone's finding that form significant, and if different persons are aesthetically responsive to different works?

But perhaps Bell doesn't see that conversely no argument could demonstrate that something was *not* a work of art, i.e. that it lacked significant form, if it provoked aesthetic emotion in someone, or, to avoid begging a question, if it provoked something which in terms of its content, was an aesthetic emotion and which was directed towards a work's arrangements of colours and lines. If he did, he could not be as patronising as he is about e.g. the 'portraiture of Holland' and those who delight in it.

So Bell's position is very narrow in its account of the nature of aesthetic emotion and value, and, though it does not follow, it is not surprising that his critical taste is also narrow and austere.[21] It is unargued, in that it assumes exactly what we are concerned with, *viz*., whether there is anything common and peculiar to works in virtue of which they have aesthetic merit; and the definition of significant form in terms of aesthetic emotion, and of aesthetic emotion in terms of significant form, is crucially circular.

Among more recent and determined attempts to establish the existence and identity of aesthetic criteria are those of Monroe Beardsley himself. Beardsley is, of course, philosophically far more sophisticated than Bell, but we shall find that his presuppositions are quite similar to Bell's and that, despite the length at which he writes, what he has to say is similarly crucially unargued. His thesis (as presented in Chapters X and XI of *Aesthetics*) runs as follows: our liking of a work of art or thinking highly of it can be justified. But this is to say that we can give reasons, and good reasons, for our view. Various sorts of reasons are offered to support such views, but those which mention its cognitive aspects or attribute moral value to it may be 'set aside', at least temporarily (pp. 456–7) leaving us with those reasons for thinking a work good, bad or better or worse, than some other work, which are peculiarly aesthetic. These in turn may be divided into three groups. There are 'genetic' reasons, 'which refer to something existing before the work itself, to the manner in which it was produced, or its connection with antecedent objects and psychological states' (p. 457). Beardsley here argues — oddly, in view of his earlier remarks that these reasons, unlike the cognitive and moral reasons, are 'peculiarly aesthetic' — that such reasons cannot be 'relevant and sound' reasons for a critical evaluation (p. 458) but we shall not discuss this claim again at this point. 'Affective' reasons are those which refer to the psychological effects of the aesthetic object upon the percipient. As Beardsley quite rightly points out, such reasons, if they do not mention the work or that aspect of the work which elicits them, tend to be vague and we could not distinguish such effects from those produced by things and events which are not aesthetic objects (p. 461). However, and perhaps surprisingly, his view is that such reasons are not aesthetically irrelevant, and indeed ultimately his account of the value of works of art is couched in terms of their effects (p. 530).

There remain 'objective' reasons, which are those which refer

to some characteristic— that is, some quality or internal relation, or set of qualities and relations— within the work itself, or to some meaning relation between the work and the world (p. 462).

In virtue of these features which define them, objective reasons are aesthetic reasons and again perhaps surprisingly these too may be divided into three groups. He writes (ibid.)

I think when we take a wide survey of critical reasons, we can find room for most of them, with very little trouble, in three main groups. First, there are reasons which seem to bear upon the degree of *unity* or disunity of the work ... Second, there are those reasons that seem to bear upon the degree of *complexity* or simplicity of the work. Third, there are those reasons that seem to bear upon the *intensity* or lack of intensity of human regional qualities in the work.

Intensity, Complexity and Unity are therefore the three pervasive criteria, the canons of aesthetic value. For it is by reference to these, and only these, that we are able to justify all the more particular evaluative principles to which we commit ourselves when we offer a relevant reason for an evaluation of an aesthetic sort.

Further evidence that this is so is provided by the nature of aesthetic experiences themselves and the ways in which they can vary in what Beardsley calls 'magnitude' (p. 529). The correct definition of 'aesthetic experience' is, as Beardsley recognises, an empirical matter, depending on how this phrase is used, and, *prima facie*, it would appear to be used of many things and in many different ways. However, Beardsley says (pp. 527–8) that the following are points on which, I take it, nearly everyone will agree: First, an aesthetic experience is one in which attention is firmly fixed upon heterogeneous but interrelated components of a phenomenally objective field . . . Second, it is an experience of some intensity . . . Third, it is an experience that hangs together, or is coherent, to an unusually high degree . . . Fourth, it is an experience that is unusually complete in itself.

Furthermore, (p. 529) one such experience may differ from another in magnitude in

three connected but independent respects: 1. it may be more *unified*, that is more coherent and/or complete, than the other; 2. its dominant quality, or pervasive feeling-tone, may be more *intensive* than that of the other; 3. the range of diversity of distinct elements that it brings together into its unity, and under its dominant quality, may be more *complex* than that of the other.

So, if it is assumed or 'granted' that aesthetic experiences are valuable, something has (instrumental) aesthetic value if it has the capacity to produce aesthetic experiences of some magnitude (p. 533) and, clearly, the greater its capacity the greater its aesthetic value.[22]

As we have observed before, the moral and intellectual dimensions of some works, as well as the skill and originality of artists who produce (or interpret) them, do play a role in eliciting and determining our aesthetic responses to and evaluations of works of art. Beardsley's definitions of 'aesthetic experiences' and 'aesthetic reasons' would explicitly seek to exclude such experiences and considerations from the realm of the aesthetic, and it would be unlikely and fortuitous if, despite this intention, these fell under his definitions.

Conversely, Beardsley's account of the aesthetic, which seeks to eliminate as irrelevant anything which might be a property of a work of art which could not be a property of a work of nature,[23] would seem artificial in another way. For it would make certain experiences which no doubt have an aesthetic dimension, for example, some sexual experiences, the very paradigm of aesthetic experiences.

If Beardsley's definition of 'aesthetic experience' is too narrow, and indeed also eccentric, then although the experiences he defines may indeed be aesthetically valuable, so may others. Similarly, he cannot prove that his canons are the only pervasive criteria of aesthetic value, or indeed pervasive criteria at all, by deriving them from an analysis of aesthetic reasons as he circumscribes them.

Were Beardsley to accept that his account of the aesthetic is too narrow, he might have to add to his canons in order to be able to show, for example, how it is that reasons he had previously excluded are aesthetically cogent. But if he were to do this to the extent that could become necessary the spirit of his thesis would evaporate. For there might be almost as many canons as reasons, but then the former could scarcely be used to demonstrate the relevance of the latter; the 'canons' would in no sense be pervasive criteria of excellence, and the unity of the aesthetic and the possibility of showing that some reasons and experiences are aesthetic, and others not, would be lost. Whether we can give a general account of the aesthetic, and whether we could derive canons of the sort that Beardsley envisages from such an account, remain open questions. What he attempts to do is not mistaken in principle, but his procedure is too *a priori*.[24]

So far we have assumed that Beardsley could derive his canons from his account of the aesthetic; and if being intense, complex and unified were constitutive of an aesthetic experience, and assuming or 'granting' that these are valuable, it would seem that there could be no problem here. Indeed, one of Beardsley's chief doubts about the canons is that they are dull[25] and 'safe' and may be 'trivial'.[26] However, he is exercised by the doubt that his canons may not really be the same in all the arts (*Aesthetics*, pp. 200–2, 208–9); if, for example, complexity were not really the same thing in painting, music and literature, he would have failed to establish that there are pervasive canons of aesthetic excellence, and would also have failed to give a general account of aesthetic experiences and reasons.

Now undoubtedly a complex painting is complex in a different way from a complex novel (and undoubtedly some complex novels are complex in different ways from other complex novels). But despite Beardsley's fears it does not follow from this that 'complex' has a different *meaning* when used of plays and novels. Indeed if this were so, 'Plays and novels are complex in different ways' would be an incoherent assertion, not a true one. At least, and at best, it would have to be an elliptical remark in which there figures what Fowler calls 'legerdemain'.[27] If 'complexity' does have a single meaning in such remarks, complexity is in the crucial and relevant way some one thing throughout the arts, though its forms vary.[28]

For Beardsley, the interesting problems with respect to aesthetic criteria arise in relation to the connection between more particular principles and his canons.

Naturally, if aesthetic enjoyment is (in part) the enjoyment of unity, unity is a ground of aesthetic value. But when the critic cites properties that are not involved in the definition of 'aesthetic enjoyment' — such as that a modulation is too abrupt, or not abrupt enough — he is giving a more interesting answer, because a synthetic connection has to be established to make the reason relevant (it must be argued that the too abrupt modulation mars the unity of the music, or that the insufficiently abrupt modulation weakens its dramatic intensity, or some other quality)'.[29]

But Beardsley's own illustration raises a problem concerning the relevance of his canons. Appeal to them could scarcely be expected to resolve a disagreement about whether a modulation is too abrupt. Nor perhaps does Beardsley think that it could (p. 539). What then the canons can do is to show that, provided a connection between them and the reasons offered by the critic can be established, his reason for his view is aesthetically *relevant*. (Of course, even if he couldn't do this, his view might nevertheless be right.) But this would scarcely seem to be a problem in the sort of case envisaged, and let us suppose instead that one critic objected to the abrupt modulation on the ground that it was too derivative, too Beethovenesque. Beardsley would say that this 'genetic' reason was irrelevant and improper.[30] But it is a fact that the aesthetic responses of people who are seriously, even professionally interested in the works they are dealing with are in part determined by what might be loosely called historical factors.[31] Beardsley would have to argue a purist line here, that although this is so, i.e. this *is* a fact about aesthetic experiences, it ought not to be so. Of course it is true that some genetic matters are irrelevant to aesthetic appreciation; but then so are some formal and intrinsic ones. Beardsley's canons do not match our intuitions (i.e. they don't square with the way in which persons seriously concerned with works of art talk about them), nor do they provide any good reasons for going against intuitions.

Consider next a similar example but one which raises yet another problem for Beardsley. Imagine two music critics disagreeing about the relative merits of two compositions, the Piano Sonata No. 23 in F minor, op. 57 (the Appassionata), by Beethoven, the movements of which are all powerful and passionate, and the Sinfonia Concertante in E Flat Major, K. 364, by Mozart, which has two exquisite first movements and a final characteristic gay movement. Again, appeal to the canons will not resolve a disagreement as to which is the better, if only because each critic *could* rationalise his preference in terms of the canons — intensity and unity for the Beethoven, a sort of complexity for the Mozart.[32] But would the critic who favours, or even simply enjoys, the Mozart choose to do this? For although in one way the Mozart is complex, and more complex than the Beethoven, it is not because it is complex that he prefers or likes it; it is rather because in ending with a gay movement, Mozart avoids the risk which Beethoven runs of being over-insistent. Mozart's doing this involves complexity, but it is not the complexity which provides the rationale for the critic's judgement, nor which creates his response to the work. Nor is this surprising, since complexity lacks any obvious *a priori* universal value of appeal. Indeed we may commend works for their exemplifying its very antithesis, *viz.*, simplicity. One of the points which is being made here is that even if when we examine a case in which the reasons adduced for a liking or preference are 'objective', the cogency of those reasons is not really explained by their bearing on or contributing to a work's complexity or necessarily on its unity, or intensity. (In the end, it might be just because Mozart avoids over-intensity that his admirers rejoice in his compositions).

The fact that, for example, complexity does lack an obvious and invariable appeal provides another problem for Beardsley's thesis that his canons show why good reasons for an aesthetic evaluation are good ones. Anyone who has an appetite and high esteem for *Anna Karenina* and *War and Peace* would mention their richness and scope. Beardsley would say that such features contribute to the work's merit because they are constitutive, in part anyway, of their great complexity.[33] But we can imagine that there might be a novel which is the equal of Tolstoy's in complexity, and that we might find that complexity no virtue at all. It would be no good Beardsley's saying that this is because the novel lacks others things which Tolstoy's has, even though this may be true, because although according to Beardsley the canons are 'connected' they are independent; complexity is in itself and by itself a virtue (p. 529; but cf. the inconsistent remarks on pp. 463–5). But it is patently less obviously a virtue than the qualities one might try to rationalise in terms of it, and it's not clear that we might always want it (or indeed richness). Yet according to Beardsley we could not have too much of it.

This is not to say that there is not a problem here. How can we commend a feature in one place and not find it praiseworthy in another? Aren't we being inconsistent and irrational if we do this? The merit of Beardsley's work is that it recognises the problem, but the thesis which he presents in *Aesthetics* and in 'The Discrimination of Aesthetic Enjoyment' totally fails to solve it.

Finally, when Beardsley gets down to trying to demonstrate the relevance of certain reasons, the argument becomes arbitrary and unconvincing, and the exercises sterile (sterile in that he conspicuously fails to demonstrate the connection, and even if he succeeded we still wouldn't be persuaded that that was why the feature in question was a merit). Presented with the quality of economy in a painting, for example, he casts around and, almost perversely it seems, places it under the canon of complexity: ' "Economy" we saw in Chapter II §S.6, can mean variety of significance in line and shape, hence a kind of complexity' (p. 467). But why complexity? Couldn't one say with equal conviction that it contributed to the work's unity or intensity or indeed to its simplicity? Beardsley's answer is that economy must 'mean' (a crucial phrase) complexity here because in another example complexity produced economy. But why should he assume that it is only complexity that could produce economy, i.e. assume that the same effect always has the same cause? In any case, this gratuitous assumption is unhelpful to Beardsley because it doesn't follow from the fact, if it is a fact, that economy is an effect of complexity, that it is itself a virtue. Beardsley may in fact be assuming the converse, *viz.*, that economy always produces complexity (same cause, same effect), and that it is therefore instrumentally good. But no evidence is produced in support of this causal thesis; and in any case, when we commend something aesthetically for its being economical we are not commending it for something else produced by that economy. Finally Beardsley may be saying not that complexity and economy stand in any causal relationship, but in a constitutive one, *viz.*, that economy involves complexity, so that if something is economical it is therefore complex.

A constitutive relationship may be substantial or conceptual, but does either exist in this case? For consider the case of a golf swing, which we find aesthetically pleasing because it is, as we say, economical. Its being economical 'means' (to use that marvellously ambiguous word) that it is simple and easy, and certainly not that in comparison with other golf swings it is or is produced by something complex.[34]

Beardsley seems curiously unaware of the nature and extent of the danger he does mention, namely that of 'freewheeling rationalisations' (p. 469). What he has in mind is the possibility that a critic might appeal to the canons improperly, exploit them to demonstrate the cogency of what he has to say. But he discounts this danger because the canons clearly exclude certain reasons, such as that a work is written by a Communist (p. 468) (though we may doubt whether such a consideration must always be irrelevant to a work's aesthetic properties or our appreciation of them). It is very doubtful if any critic would feel the need to try to rationalise the reasons he adduces in terms of Beardsley's canons, and the more real dangers of rationalisations are the ones that these terms permit Beardsley.

Beardsley's search to establish canons fails. We may now feel persuaded that any such attempt would fail, because there are no canons.

It follows from this that at no level of abstraction are there considerations or reasons of a sort to which we must always allude, if only implicitly, if a judgement we make is to be an aesthetically evaluative and a correct one. (Nor are there considerations or reasons which are sufficient to ensure this.) Instead, what we say in explaining and defending such judgements may, and usually does, differ not only from art form to art form, but within the art forms from case to case.

Of course even if there were no aesthetic criteria of any sort, universal or local, it might nonetheless be true that *in fact* all men had similar aesthetic likes and so values; but of course they do not. Some like one thing, others not. So the view that in fact, *really*, men do all enjoy and value the same aesthetic properties in objects could be correct only if it were the case that everyone *would* enjoy and prefer the same works of art, or have the same aesthetic responses to objects, if they were all equally aware of the aesthetic properties of those objects.

But again it seems clear that there are occasions on which two persons are equally and similarly aware of the features of some work, yet respond to and value them, and the works, differently. If it is now said, 'But where aesthetic responses are similar, then there is no difference in likings or estimations of worth', that is only true if the responses in question indicate liking or estimations of worth, in which case the claim becomes vacuous — or at least untestable.[35] Moreover the truth of this vacuous thesis is itself consistent with there being nothing in common, and peculiar, to these common responses to differing objects. In any case, the differences between the responses of individuals to particular objects remain.

If these observations are correct, then aesthetic judgements of value, and aesthetic objects which are valued, lack an essence. And so too, no doubt, do aesthetic objects, i.e., works of art, or objects viewed aesthetically, as indeed does the 'aesthetic view'. To say this is not to deny that, for example, to 'view something aesthetically', involves taking up a characteristic attitude to something, or that works of art have much in common with each other which they do not share with other objects.

But the conclusion that aesthetic judgements of value, aesthetic judgements, and aesthetic objects lack an essence should not surprise or dismay us. If Wittgenstein is right mathematics too lacks an essence, and gets on perfectly well without one; and the feeling that mathematics must have an essence would seem more powerful and better grounded than a parallel view for art.

Beardsley's belief that art and aesthetic judgements must have an essence appears to have two sources, beyond the fact that there is a common core of response and judgement. First, the belief held by Bell and many others that where we have one word, in this case 'art', all that to which the term applies must at some level of abstraction be one thing. Secondly, there is the feeling that unless this is so we would not be able to distinguish aesthetic objects from other objects, aesthetic reasons from other reasons, or indeed good aesthetic reasons from ones which are not good.

But there is no reason for thinking that any of these putative conclusions follow. It would only be if a critic might appropriately say *anything* in explaining and defending his aesthetic judgement and if what he said in one case had no implications whatsoever for what he might say in another that there would be cause to feel that criticism is either arbitrary or irrational.

5 Reasons, causes and targets

Beardsley has defended a less extreme and more plausible position than the one previously discussed, based on his view that we do advance reasons, and good ones sometimes, and that these, being reasons, must be general. Other aestheticians[1] take precisely the opposite view of critical remarks, *viz*., that they are logically singular (though they deny the apparent consequences). Our reader will by now be familiar with our belief that neither of these monlithic views can be right. In this final chapter we shall try to show why, by a critique of these two views, and also why this rejection of extremes, far from leaving us floundering in a sea of criticism, better equips us to deal appropriately with each fresh wave.

In perhaps his best known discussion of questions concerning criteria in criticism, Beardsley defends what he calls the 'General Criterion Theory' (the 'G.C.T.') against attacks from those he calls the 'Critical Skeptics'. The Critical Skeptic believes that 'no good or cogent reasons can be given for critical judgements'.[2] Beardsley rightly observes that critical skepticism has various grounds and parts, but the denial of the theory that there are *general* criteria to support critical judgements is one part of critical skepticism. Why should the critical skeptic deny this? Beardsley considers, and attempts to rebut, four arguments which have been adduced by various sceptical critics.

The first is that the G.C.T. can't be true because there are no single features of, for example, poetry that are either necessary or sufficient for goodness. (This, says Beardsley, seems to be the main point of Pleydell-Pearce's 'On the Limits and Use of "Aesthetic Criteria" ', *Philosophical Quarterly* (1959).) Beardsley here accepts that there is no single sufficient feature of goodness in poetry and also concedes 'for the sake of argument' that there is no single feature which is necessary either, though in fact he believes that coherence is such a condition. But, he asks, what follows? It may still be true that there exist certain features of poetry such that wherever one of these features is found in a poem it may contribute to the goodness of that poem, and, thus, may be citable as a merit wherever it can be found. Indeed, magnanimity is just such a feature of moral worth.

A second argument (which Beardsley finds in W.E. Kennick's 'Does Traditional Aesthetics Rest on a Mistake?', *Mind* (1958)) is that certain features of works of art, e.g., humour or tragic intensity, may be merits 'in different contexts'. He attempts to rebut this rather unclearly stated objection by saying such features may always be good things when they can be had— only it may turn out that they cannot all be had in the same work, 'or not without being watered down or confused'. Although Beardsley's point here is a valid one, for certain features of works of art which we value may indeed be mutually incompatible, it does not exactly meet the sceptic's argument that there are features of works which we value in some works, but which we do not value, or which we feel are actual defects, when we find them elsewhere.

That certain features may be merits in some works but not merits — but not defects either — in others is the third argument of the critical sceptic (which Beardsley again attributes to Kennick) and he answers it by pointing out that some features of poems may contribute value 'so to speak on their own, while others do so only in combination'. But again, this fact, if it is a fact, about works of art does not tell against the G.C.T. Beardsley does not argue this claim, but its justification would perhaps be that the incompatible and fruitful combinations would be incompatible and fruitful wherever they appear.

The fourth argument is an extension of the third according to Beardsley, though we found it in the second. It is that some features may be 'merits in one work and actually defects in another'. Beardsley concedes this possibility but says that the G.C.T. can meet the difficulty by one more complication 'that is natural and sensible'. All it needs to assume is that there are two different sorts of feature of works of art: primary (positive) criteria, which are always merits in that the addition or increase of such a feature, without any decrease in the other primary criteria, will always make the work better; and secondary criteria, which sometimes contribute to the existence of the primary ones, when they are virtues, but sometimes work against their existence, when they are defects. Moreover, they do so in a systematic general way, even though a particular combination of features may exist only in one work of art.

Now Beardsley does not appear, or claim, to attempt to establish the claims he makes about works of art in defence of the G.C.T.; what he says about the relationship between features of works of art and their merit is plausible and the illustrations he gives are convincing. But this falls short of proof, for which it would seem an *a priori* argument would be needed (to exclude the *possibility* of counter-examples to his defence). He is only concerned to demonstrate that though the observations which lead sceptical critics to attack the G.C.T. may be true, the G.C.T. may yet be true.

But is it true? What would have to be the case if it were false? Or, to ask a similar question in a different way, why does Beardsley feel that the theory that there are *general* criteria to support critical judgements must be right? He assumes that the critic does make value judgements and 'does sometimes adequately support them by good reasons' and his argument is then as follows:

If one proposition is a reason for another, in the sense of actually supporting it, then there must be a logical connection of some sort between them. And, being a logical connection, it must relate general concepts in an abstract way . . . Some philosophers, including Mr. Kennick, hold that we can still talk of giving reasons in particular cases (that is, supporting the judgement that this or that poem is good or poor), without committing ourselves to any general principles at all. Others, however, hold (and I think with more reason) that some form of generality is essential to reason giving and, therefore, that if there are no general criteria, there can be no critical criteria at all.

And last, and perhaps most illuminatingly,

Speaking very sketchily, I conceive the peculiar aesthetic goodness of a work of art to consist of its capacity to provide experiences with certain desirable qualities; and the criteria of critical evaluation are simply features that tend to contribute to or detract from this capacity. Hence, according to my theory, there is a causal relationship involved in the notion of critical criteria. And since I side with those who think that some generalised lawful relationships are essential to individual causal actions, by the same token I must suppose that a criterion can be relevant to the value of a particular work of art only if some generality of bearing lurks (so to speak) in the background.

Here we have the *a priori* considerations which explain Beardsley's commitment to the generality of critical criteria. *Caeteris paribus*, the same cause must produce the same effect. And if our reason for thinking a work good is that it has some feature which, perhaps in combination with other features of the work, has the capacity to produce certain desirable experiences, then we are committed at least to the claim that if that feature occurs in some other work in combination with similar features, that work will also and for the same reason be good.

Such considerations may strike us as being at once both ungainsayable and irrelevant; with a little tightening up, perhaps they must be true, and yet they do not seem to have any application to the business of criticism. Why? Someone who, like Kennick, denies that critical criteria are general, may not deny the 'same cause, same effect' thesis. His grounds for denying their generality may be that the notion of 'same cause' never has application in art. For works of art are not always simply different, but different in respect of our appreciation of them.[3]

But Beardsley, understandably, sees it as no objection to his thesis that it has no immediate application when formulated in terms of 'same cause, same effect'. For another formulation of the thesis is that differences between works will systematically determine our different responses to, and hence our evaluations of them.[4]

The 'sceptical critic' may also be impressed by the fact that works of art are very complex. Partly for this reason, and also because he may feel that Beardsley's thesis concerning criteria would turn the critic into a quasi-scientist, and an ignorant and slovenly one at that, he will point out that as critics we are ignorant of the causal laws which connect the critical works of art with our responses to them, i.e., their 'effects', even if there are such laws. Nonetheless, we are not ignorant of the works themselves, or of how we respond to them, our experience of them. Hence, we do know in particular cases what we are responding to and, in some sense of 'why', why we respond as we do. Indeed, it is the proper business of the critic, as opposed, for example to the linguist, to articulate our experience of particular works, not to make scientific discoveries concerning what produces it. And while such discussions may be of interest to the scientist, they are irrelevant to criticism, for they could not correct appreciation or enhance its expression.[5]

But this reply leaves us with several questions. We may know what our responses are, and at some gross level what we are responding to as critics; but can we know what is producing our responses, and how, if we are ignorant of these causal laws? Johnson's experiment[6] was not irrelevant and the questions we asked concerning some of Ricks' comments are not irrelevant either. The critic is no scientist, and when he not only explains but justifies his explanation of a work, or some feature of it, he may be 'adducing reasons' rather than discovering causes. But causes and reasons are not wholly distinct. If in explaining and justifying his high estimation of a line of poetry a critic mentions its assonance, must the line not be assonant, and must it not be the assonance which is 'doing the work', i.e., producing the valuable experience, if his reason is to be correct? Giving the correct reason for a judgement may involve citing a cause, and failure to cite what is in fact a cause may produce a mere rationalisation. In any case, reasons — and rationalisations — just like causal judgements, would seem to involve what Beardsley called 'general concepts'.

Someone sympathetic to Bearsley's general position on this question of generality might also point out that, whatever the answers to the above questions, if and to the extent that we do say that a work is good because of some experience it can afford us (whatever feature does this, and however it does it) must we not be committing ourselves to general *normative* claims? Surely at very least we must be committing ourselves to the claim that the experience in question and *others like it* are valuable and, hence, so are the works capable of producing them? (Beardsley fails to make this point since he characterises critical criteria in terms of the features which produce such valuable experiences rather than the experiences themselves. But if we are ignorant of exactly what it is that produces these experiences, and it is these experiences that are valuable, our judgement that a certain feature in a work is valuable will be a more or less risky inferential judgement and the value placed on the feature will be instrumental.)

However, the generality of such normative claims as 'This is valuable (and so of course is anything like it)', is quite specious. And Kennick and others may insist that our normative knowledge when we are doing criticism is itself always singular.[7] A certain degree of sharpness may be a general criterion of merit in knives,[8] but no such connection is known or believed to exist between, say, Pope's wit and poetry. Yet it is this which the critic mentions in giving an account of the merits of that poet's verse.

What, then, if any, are the generalising implications of such critical remarks as 'It is, perhaps, chiefly his wit that we value in Pope's poetry'? That Pope's wit is and so, *a fortiori*, wit can be, a virtue in poetry? But this surely is too weak a generalisation to support the thesis that critical criteria are general. Or might it be that Pope's wit is a virtue in his poetry and therefore, such wit must be, *caeteris paribus*, a virtue wherever it appears? Again, this seems too weak a generalisation to support the point at issue, and yet, again, it sounds fishy. Pope's wit— or, to avoid begging a question, poetical wit like Pope's — could not simply be tacked on to other verse; but, no doubt, the *caeteris paribus* clause takes care of this difficulty. But how about the difficulty that in art we can have too much of a good thing (even from one author)?

Perhaps what Beardsley would want to hang on to is this: that 'Pope's wit' must be characterisable in general terms and that whenever it, or anything like it appears we can recognise it, respond to it, and say, again in general terms, why it is a virtue (when it *is* a virtue. And when it is not we should again be able to say, in general terms, why it is not.) For unless this is true, our responses to art are fortuitous, accidental, or capricious, and our evaluations of them will be arbitrary, and inarticulable.

But might it not be the case that at least some phrases like 'Pope's wit' can only be defined ostensively, via examples? And might these bear no more than a 'family resemblance'? And might it not also be the case that, in certain cases anyway, we may be unable to say why certain features of works of art, or the experiences they afford, are valuable? (Such a suggestion need not be obscurantist or depressing. For what would it be *like* to have answers to such questions as 'Why do we value the experience of hitting a cricket ball on the meat of the bat? Why does this experience feel good?' One should remember that here a 'scientific' answer would be irrelevant.)

We can now begin to see why some philosophers of criticism, and critics too, want to insist that the concepts used in criticism are not general. We can also begin to see why it is that some of them believe that to talk of our responses to works of art, our experience of them, as effects, and the works themselves, or their features, as causes gets this relation between us and art wrong. Thus if responses were merely effects then it would in principle be possible for something quite other than the work itself to produce these 'effects', e.g., a drug, but our response is *to* the work and our interest in a work is not merely instrumental as Beardsley's position implies.

We have already touched on the question of whether responses to works of art are effects of them or not; and the difficulties which attach to construing aesthetic responses as effects of works of art are almost entirely removed by the realisation that works of art are also characteristically the target of these responses, i.e., that to which our emotions, thoughts and feelings are directed. Once we appreciate this point the bogey of instrumentalism which attaches to saying that aesthetic responses are effects of works of art simply disappears, and so does the other big fear, that our responses can only be described and explained in a scientific way. But when we attempt the critical task of, for example, explaining why something is funny, we shall characteristically adduce reasons in which we mention such features in the work as certain incongruities, invention, wit, etc., that is, features which work on us intellectually and emotionally, and of whose working on us we can be intellectually aware.[9] But in insisting that these features work on us, that our responses to works are also effects of them, we allow for the possibility, for which we must allow, that our critical account can miss the mark, can be an incorrect but sometimes extremely plausible rationalisation. It is because our responses are characteristically both effects of works of art and directed towards the work or a particular feature of it that we are able to say truthfully, and in that sense rightly, that what, for example, we are laughing at is some incongruity in a central character, and then discover, no doubt to our surprise and embarrassment, that we do not find this funny unless we are aware of an audience which is also laughing.[10] Or alternatively, and perhaps more characteristically, we may read a critic who says that it is not *that* feature which is funny but *this* one. We are then involved in the problematic mental exercise of trying to determine what is doing the work. It is sheer philistinism to think that causal questions are not raised here, that experiment may not be involved in cases of this sort (e.g. showing a film without its background music, masking parts of frames to exclude a certain character), just as it is philistinism to think that experiments are always appropriate, and even when appropriate possible.[11]

What we are getting towards here is a very general explanation of why it is that criticism is an art, rather than a science, but not one in which the correctness and value of what the practitioner does is always and immediately determined by how people respond to what he says.

Now finally, we should look at an article by Arnold Isenberg,[12] for he appreciates that the Beardsley type of account of criticism seems quite unreal, but is also aware that it is the account we think must be right on *a priori* grounds; in consequence he entirely rejects it and puts forward a thesis in which all critical judgements are singular. The main concern of this article is not so much with the validity or objectivity of critical judgements, but rather with their function and import.

It begins with a statement of the theory of criticism which is to be demolished. This theory divides the critical process into three parts.

There is the value judgement or *verdict* (V): 'This picture or poem is good ——'. There is a particular statement or *reason* (R): '—— because it has such-and-such a quality (Q) ——'. And there is a general statement or *norm* (N): '—— and any work which has that quality is *pro tanto* good.'

Isenberg notes *en passant* that the circumscription of R depends on circumstances. That is to say, as against Beardsley, nothing can be ruled out as an aesthetic reason or judgement *a priori*. Isenberg notices that V and R are often combined in one remark and their connection is a problem but one which he will not consider. 'We shall be concerned solely with the descriptive function of R.'

Isenberg goes on to ask what makes a description critically useful and relevant. The first suggestion is that it is supported by N. N, according to Isenberg, is based upon an inductive generalisation which describes a relationship between some aesthetic quality and someone's or everyone's system of aesthetic response. But it is not itself an inductive generalisation, for N is not being used to *predict or explain* anybody's reaction to a work but to *vindicate* that reaction.

However, there are considerations, Isenberg feels, which permit us to dismiss N altogether; that is, it has no role to play in criticism. What are these considerations? Isenberg begins his attack on the model by 'reminding' the reader of the difference between *explaining* and *justifying* a critical response. If a psychologist should be asked 'Why X likes the object y' he would take X's enjoyment as a datum, a fact to be explained.

And if he offers as explanation the presence in y of the quality Q, there is, explicit or latent in his causal argument, an appeal to some generalization which he has reason to think is true, such as "X likes any work which has that quality". But when we ask X as a critic "why he likes the object y", we want him to give us some reason to like it too and are not concerned with the causes of what we may so far regard as his bad taste.

Why is this distinction between genetic and normative enquiry commonly ignored, Isenberg asks, 'in the practice of aesthetic speculation'? Partly because 'Why do you like this work?' is ambiguous (and why, we might ask, is that so?), but mainly because some statements about the object will necessarily figure both in the explanation and in the critical defence of any reaction to it. So, Isenberg says, if he tried to *explain* his feeling for the line

But musical as is Apollo's lute

he would certainly mention 'the pattern of u's and l's which reinforces the meaning with its own musical quality', for this quality of his sensations, he remarks, is doubtless among the conditions of his 'feeling response'. However, if he wished to convince another of the beauty of the line he would say the same thing. 'The remark which gives a reason also, in this case, states a cause.'

But, Isenberg says, though as criticism this comment might be very effective, it is practically worthless as explanation (though construed causally he thinks it true). For we have no phonetic or psychological laws nor any plausible 'common sense' generalisations from which we might derive the prediction that such a pattern of u's and l's should be pleasing to him or to anyone else. (So, construed causally, the remark is probably true, seems plausible, but, since it does not take us beyond the particular case, provides a very low-level 'explanation' of the response in this case.) In fact, the formulation is so vague that one could not tell just what general hypothesis it is that is being invoked or assumed. Yet, he says, it is quite sharp enough for critical purposes. For let us suppose that someone should fail to be convinced by Isenberg's argument for Milton's line. He might still readily admit that the quality which Isenberg mentioned (the pattern of u's and l's) might have something to do with Isenberg's pleasurable reaction, given his peculiar mentality.

Isenberg's objections to construing R causally then are that if thus construed, R and other such remarks fail to commit us to any specific or specifiable causal generalisations, and even if they did do so, we would not know whether the generalisations were true. Moreover, even if these generalisations were true, and known to be true, they would not forward critical discussion and would be irrelevant. For the question is not what causes one's, perhaps peculiar or defective, response, but how should one respond? And to answer this question a critically relevant observation might well mention something in the work which has not played a role in determining someone's response. So Isenberg does not deny the need for sound inductive generalisations in aesthetic explanation, but he maintains that the correct understanding of critical remarks does not commit us to them.

But if we are committed to N in producing R, what is the role, function or import of N? Isenberg denies it any; and so, he observes, have others, but they have done so for the wrong reasons. Thus one group— like Isenberg— say that they know of no law which governs human tastes and preferences, no quality shared by any two works that makes them attractive or repellent. But, says Isenberg, this assumes that if N were based on a sound generalisation, N, together with R, would be a real ground for the acceptance of V, so that according to this objection criticism is being held back by the miserable state of aesthetic science. 'This raises an issue too large to be canvassed here', remarks Isenberg; but his objection to this group, who are surely guilty of a sort of crude populism or naturalistic fallacy, is that some critical judgements have been 'proved' as well as in the nature of the case they can be proved. So the validation of critical judgements cannot wait on the discovery of aesthetic laws. Moreover, to the extent that there are such laws (known or unknown) there is that much less disagreement in criticism. But discovering them could not help to resolve *disagreements*. 'We are not more fully convinced in our judgement because we know its explanation, and we cannot hope to convince an imaginary opponent by an appeal to this explanation which by hypothesis does not hold for him.' Really then Isenberg treats these persons as construing N as a causal generalisation.

The second more radical group deny N a function on the

grounds that the very excuse for the existence of a work of art lies in its difference from everything that has gone before. We do not judge it in terms of its resemblance to other works. Croce *et al* wish to deny any notion of a standard whatsoever, but they fail to provide any positive interpretation of criticism. For *all* criticism, bad and good, cites as reasons for praising or condemning a work one or more of its qualities. So if the descriptive reasons are true, how can we object to bad criticism except by objecting to the critic's standards? The appearance of seeming to relapse into a reliance upon standards is unavoidable as long as we have no alternative interpretation of the function and import of R: either it is arbitrary or it presupposes and depends on some general claim.

The task then is to give a correct account of the function and import of R. Isenberg attempts this by looking at a piece of art appreciation in which the critic mentions the outline of figures in a painting, using the phrase 'the contour of a violently rising and falling wave'. (Remember that in doing this he is justifying a favourable judgement.) Now, asks Isenberg, is the critic to be construed as telling us of the presence in the painting of a steeply rising and falling curve? He says *not*, because this same quality (a steeply rising and falling curve) could be found in any of a hundred lines one could draw on a board in three minutes, and also because it could not be the critic's purpose to inform us of the presence of any quality as obvious as this.

So, according to Isenberg, the critic must be thinking of another quality, no idea of which is transmitted by his language, which he sees and which by his use of language he gets us to see. This quality is a wavelike contour, but it is not the quality designated by the expression 'wavelike contour'. The phrase excludes many things and yet gives no directions for perceiving what the critic is interested in. The critic's *meaning* is 'filled in', 'rounded out' by the act of perception which is performed not to judge the truth of his description but in a certain sense to *understand* it. It is a function of criticism to bring about communication at the level of the senses; that is, to induce a sameness of vision, of experienced content. With scientific prose, experience is necessary for understanding the simple terms; with criticism this is always necessary. Hence, 'reading criticism, otherwise than in the presence, or with direct recollection, of the objects discussed is a blank and senseless occupation . . .'. He continues 'There is not in all the world's criticism a single descriptive statement concerning which one is prepared to say beforehand "If it is true, I shall like the work so much the better." ' And why is this? The reason is, of course, that we do not know what the critic is talking about, i.e. which quality in the work he likes and is drawing attention to, until after we have seen the work and seen what he is talking about. Isenberg continues 'the truth of R never adds the slightest weight to V, because R does not designate any quality the perception of which might induce us to assent to V . . . . The critic is not committed to the general claim that the quality named Q is valuable because he never makes the particular claim that a work is good in virtue of the presence of Q'.

Now Isenberg's claim, that a central function of the critic is to sensitise his audience to the presence of qualities in the work whose precise nature is what is important, which is not specified by the very meaning of the phrase, and whose effect cannot, perhaps, be predicted in other contexts, is often right. But surely the critic can and does build up a critical vocabulary by which he identifies certain qualities which can recur and which, when they do, he can identify, cf. 'Rembrandt's chiaroscuro', 'Pope's wit', 'El Greco's flame-like line', etc. Now as the occurrence of proper names in them indicates, just what the qualities which these terms designate are like can, no doubt, only be learned through experience, ostensively. But if they are indeed valuable — and they are — why is the critic not committed to any general claim, if indeed he is not? It is not, as Isenberg thinks, because the critic never makes the particular claim that a work is good in virtue of the presence of Q. *He is doing just that when the above, and other, phrases are substituted for 'Q' in R.* No; it is rather because Q itself, though always the same thing, will also exhibit differences which may be important for our appreciation; this becomes particularly clear when we remember that our appreciation of, say, Pope's wit, however instantly recognisable that phenomenon is, may be — indeed it is and we know this — a function of, among other things, the subject matter of the poem, and many other variables. Moreover, and we have noticed this before, the qualities we respond to as we respond to them are often linked to their authorship, so if that is different, and we know this, the quality, and our responses to it, may be different. If a critic does not commit himself to general claims it is because works of art are so complex, and not because he never makes a particular claim that a work is good in virtue of the presence of a quality mentioned in his remark.

A wise critic will therefore be careful and tentative, but this doesn't mean that he would never commit himself to general claims. A committed critic might say, truthfully, and indeed rightly, that he is very unlikely to think well of a work which seems to argue against a greater social equality in the world. A director may say that he's not interested in, he has no time for, he is contemptuous of, plays which require for their success the unwilling and embarrassed cooperation of members of the audience.[13] A critic may say that he thinks it very likely that to the extent that a novel does not 'tell the truth' he will think the less of it. And it would be absurd to think that critics cannot and so do not commit themselves to such general claims because, of course, they may be overthrown by some future experience. If this reasoning were valid one would have to say that one could not commit oneself to any general claim even in science. The difference between criticism and science, then, in the matter of prediction is not that a critic never predicts, never commits himself to general explanatory claims; he does, (think yet again of the effect of the minor key). It is just that he does so less often and more tentatively than the scientist.

As for Isenberg's illustrative example, it may be precisely that wavelike contour which could indeed be found in any of a hundred lines one could draw on the board in three minutes which is valuable *in that painting*. There is in Glasgow[14] a painting attributed to Giorgione, 'Christ and the Woman Taken in Adultery', which, given the attribution, is surprisingly badly composed. There is a disproportionately large amount of foreground, a line of figures wanders away to the right, and our attention wanders inappropriately to this periphery of the painting. But it seems likely that the painting is mutilated, and that in its original condition, a copy of which is reproduced in the gallery, a strong figure stands to the right. Here we can perform a simple experiment which shows that the effect of this figure, which is in part no doubt an effect of the resulting arc of the line of feet, is to draw our eye back and forth along the arc of figures thus restoring Christ as the appropriate focus of the work. Yet the line of feet describes a quite mundane arc which could no doubt be drawn on a board many times in three minutes.

It is also naive of Isenberg to think that the features or qualities of works of art which the critic may appropriately mention can not be obvious; it is rather that they are frequently not obvious to us until after the critic has drawn our attention to them. Jane Austen's serious moral concern, for example, is something the young reader characteristically misses, but once he sees it, it is obvious; similarly with Lawrence's intelligence as a critic, to which someone might be blinded by a dislike of his novels.

Our ignorance of general laws fills our lives, but this should not drive us into as it were an obscurantist analysis of many of the things we say. For example, I might say accusingly. 'You knocked me over,' and that may well be true, and is true if, *caeteris paribus*, I wouldn't have fallen over had you not bumped into me. But how do I know that? Well, I *felt* you push me over, and I have moral certainty here, and that depends on my experience of life. Nonetheless, in claiming that you knocked me over I am, no doubt, committed to general claims about the relations of masses and velocities and centres of gravity; but I may be ignorant of these laws while morally certain about the truth of the particular statement.

This point returns us to a mistake that Isenberg makes at the beginning of his article. He say, quite rightly, that any ostensibly singular claim, construed causally, commits the claimant to general laws, and argues that since we are ignorant of these in connection with the affairs of criticism, the singular claims made by the critic ought not to be construed causally; and if they are so construed the explanation which they give of the critic's response is a very low level one. Well, that is true, but as we have seen with the previous example it may be quite sufficient for our purposes, and appropriate for our state of knowledge and our interest in the matter in hand. Of course a science of aesthetic response would not achieve a greater community of judgement than already exists, but insofar as we had it, it would give us a check on what forms a large part of criticism, namely the explanation and, since that warrants the response, the justification of a critic's likings. If we had a science of aesthetic response — and we have already shown why that science would have to be incomplete — we would have a check on what in another context Beardsley called 'freewheeling rationalisations'. And if these remarks sound too 'scientifically' orientated, we need only remind ourselves that such a science would have nothing to say about what for much criticism is the central matter, namely 'what ought we to like?'

It is because critics misunderstand their own activity, according to Isenberg, that, when they disagree, one critic will take another's remarks at 'face value' and try to show that 'by those standards' (whatever Q the other has mentioned), some other valued work would have to be condemned. He may even, he says, attempt an experiment and, to show that his opponent's grounds are irrelevant, construct a travesty of the original poem in which whatever has been approved is held constant while the rest is changed. But Isenberg says, this is to assume that the critic's function is to explain experiences rather than to clarify and alter them. And if we saw that 'the *meaning* of a word like "assonance" — the quality which it leads our perception to discriminate in one poem or another— is in critical usage never twice the same', we would see no point in 'testing' any generalisation about the relationship between assonance and poetic value.

But Isenberg simply assumes here that a critic can never make a mistake, or learn from another who employs experiment or a comparative procedure. Yet a critic might give an account, a justification, of his liking of, for example, Donne's 'Death be not proud' in terms of Donne's characteristic use of paradox. Another critic may come along and point out that 'The Legacie' similarly depends on paradox but, doesn't the other agree, 'The Legacie' doesn't come off? And the first critic may have to agree. Or again, a critic might explain, justify, locate his liking for 'The Extasie' in terms of its use of complex argument, but be led to see that similarly complex argument occurs in the inferior 'Lovers Infinitenesse'. And this procedure in the hands of a critic like Leavis can lead us not merely to relocate and recharacterise our liking of a work but to give it up. In other words, a critical term like 'assonance' can and often does have the same literal meaning from one bit of criticism to another, and the assonance itself can be very similar in the two cases, and the comparative method can lead us to see that perhaps it was not the assonance which gave the first work its merit, which explained our liking; and our liking too can be dissipated in this manner.

Isenberg is committed to the view that to ask 'But how about *this*? Doesn't this have assonance (or whatever) too?' is an *ignoratio* in criticism.[15] But it need not be. And his own account of critical remarks has two consequences: he can give no intelligible account of the semantic relation between critical terms and features in the works to which they are applied; secondly, because he wants to make critical judgements not only absolutely particular to the work discussed but completely without causal dimension, he can give no account of how a critic might be wrong, or yet of course how he might be right, in locating that in the work which has merit (cf. his Note pp. 154–5). As perhaps the final paragraph of his Note indicates, had Isenberg realised that cause and target may and characteristically do coincide in aesthetic responses, his seeing that critical remarks are often sensitising and characterising would not have led him to deny their causal, contingent, and generalising dimension.

In conclusion: in this book we have striven to show that criticism is enormously various, is characteristically both highly complex and problematic, the latter particularly when it strikes us as being most interesting and informative. One of our major efforts has been to show why though it cannot be treated as a science, and perhaps a failed one, with a normative dimension tagged on, neither can it be treated as something *sui generis*, mysterious, whose truths are only apprehended, never proved, and in which an analytic examination of their basis is scarcely possible and in any case inappropriate because irrelevant.

We hope that the effect of this book will be to sharpen and deepen the critic's appreciation of these points, the more disturbing of which, we have noticed, he will sometimes acknowledge with the lips but rather more rarely with the heart; and we hope too that, without making criticism tedious, an effect of our work might be to help to make it more self-aware and self-critical.

Acknowledgements

We are grateful to Professor Christopher Ricks for permission to reprint an extract from the Introduction to *Poems and Critics* (Collins, 1966).

Versions of some sections of this book have been published as articles. We are grateful to the following for permission to reprint these: the Editor of the *Journal of Aesthetics and Art Criticism*, and the American Society of Aesthetics, for 'The Complexity of Criticism; its Logic and Rhetoric'; the Editor of *Mind* for Colin Radford's 'A Causal Judgement in Criticism'; and the Editor of *Southern Review* for Colin Radfords 'Critical Arguments'.

Notes

Introduction

1. The high esteem in which Dickens is now held by literary critics is to some extent the result of their belated struggle to come to terms with the general and persistent taste for his work. That struggle is aptly described by John Middleton Murry, writing at a time when it had not yet come to fruition:

   > Dickens is a baffling figure. There are moments when it seems his chief purpose in writing was to put a spoke in the wheel of our literary aesthetics. We manage to include everybody but him; and we are inclined in our salad days to resent the existence of anybody who refuses to enter the scheme. That is why people tried to get rid of him by declaring that he was not an artist. It was an odd way of predicating non-existence. Now it is going out of fashion, I suppose because it did not have the desired effect of annihilating Dickens; and also perhaps because simple people asked why the books of a man who was not an artist should have this curious trick of immortality. There was, alas, no answer. So we are beginning to discover that Dickens *was* an artist, but, of course, only in parts. When we have discovered which are the parts we shall breathe again.

   > John Middleton Murry *Pencillings* (London, 1923) pp. 40–1

2. We find the whole range of implied 'should's' in *Hamlet* criticism. A critic such as B.L. Joseph sees the *accurate* reading as the only proper one to take; if we are to read the text as it should be read, we must see Hamlet as a revenge tragedy:

   > We are not concerned with what seems sensible today, but with what the Elizabethan playgoer accepted as sensible. We can, for instance, be certain he would not have asked, like some modern readers, what was the use of killing Claudius, how could that have saved Gertrude's honour? A society in which duelling was so prevalent as to alarm the Privy Council, instead of asking such questions knew that in a revenge play a nobleman was bound to kill Claudius . . .

   > B.L. Joseph, *Conscience and the King* (London, 1968), p. 24

   A critic like L.C. Knights, however, takes the opposite view — the only way to read Hamlet properly is from the right moral viewpoint, and so according to him, we should read the play as a Christian tragedy: of the passage, 'It faded on the crowing of the cock', he takes the tone of the whole play:

161

Here, in the passage before us, not only is Christmas night whole-
some, hallowed and gracious, because various malign influences are
as powerless to act as spirits such as this are to stir abroad; but also
the limpid freshness of the verse emphasises an accepted Christianity
which, it seems in place to remark, is directly opposed to the code of
revenge.

> L.C. Knights, *An Approach to Hamlet* (London, 1960), p. 45

A third, perhaps more moderate, view is taken by critics such as S. de
Madariaga, who says that the 'proper' way to read the text is as any
intelligent and sensitive man would naturally read it, without preconceptions; to do this, he says, we should take our key to the play from our
response to Hamlet himself:

There is no mystery about *Hamlet*. Once the film of prejudice and
misinterpretation is removed, the play stands perfectly clear, and its
chief character, solidly built on sound psychological premises, is
treated with all the freedom and subtle mastery of true creative
genius.

> S. de Madariaga, *On Hamlet* (London, 1948), p. 107

Many critics are, of course, less dogmatic. They are finding their way as
much as we are and perhaps we find them more helpful than the
hard-line critics. But whatever *Hamlet* critic we look at we will almost
certainly find that they have some sense of the 'proper' way to approach
the work.

3. For a discussion on this see Colin Radford, 'Characterising-Judgements
   and their Causal Counterparts', *Analysis*, January 1971, pp. 65–75
4. F.R. Leavis sums up this view of literature in specific reference to the
   novel:

   Is there any great novelist whose preoccupation with 'form' is not a
   matter of his responsibility towards a rich human interest, or complexity of interests, profoundly realised? — a responsibility involving, of its very nature, imaginative sympathy, moral discrimination,
   and judgement of relative human value?

   > F.R. Leavis, *The Great Tradition* (London, 1960), p. 29

   Dr. Johnson makes the same claim about Shakespeare:

   It may be said that he has not only shown human nature as it acts in
   real exigencies, but as it would be found in trials to which it cannot
   be exposed.

   > *Preface to Shakespeare, Works of Samuel Johnson,* Yale edition ed. A.
   > Sherbo (1968), Vol. VII.

   And the claim does not apply only to literature; we will find it in any
   sensitive criticism of, for example, Michelangelo, or Beethoven.
5. Although, given our recognition of the centrality of art in our lives, we

may find an intelligent man's complete lack of interest in art equally puzzling.

6.　　The confidence of his paraphrase made me open my eyes. It is a philosopher's confidence — the confidence of one who, in the double strength of a philosophic training and a knowledge of Blake's system ignores the working of poetry.

F.R. Leavis, 'Literary Criticism and Philosophy', *Scrutiny,* Vol. VI, 1937. Reprinted in *The Common Pursuit* (London, 1952).

Chapter 1: The complexities of critical judgements

1. Hamlet's plight is not the result of *hamartia* — it is caused by the situation he finds himself in, which is not of his doing, and his consequent state of mind. Aristotle might argue that his *hamartia* consisted in his not killing Claudius immediately — but wouldn't seeing the play in this way lessen its tragic status for us?
2. Aristotle, *Poetics*, trans. T.S. Dorsch (Penguin, London 1965), p. 48
3. A. MacIntyre, *A Short History of Ethics* (New York, 1966), pp. 5–13
4. At least, good within the terms of their genre. The fact that people laugh at a Whitehall farce does not mean that it is a *good* play — it might seem crass in comparison with a Restoration comedy — but it does mean that it is a good *farce.*
5. There must be a splendid fit between 'Ten green bottles . . .' and the situation of drunken troops fighting in the Mons trenches during the First World War. Had they sung this song, its deeper significance would be unarguable. But they did not do so — nor did any men similarly placed; it is simply a nonsense song in spite of this potential 'fit'.
6. One might put this in terms of meaning because anyone who understands the language can't deny it.
7. See. F. Bowers, *Elizabethan Revenge Tragedy, 1587—1642* (Princeton, 1940), and L.P.S. Conklin, *Hamlet Criticism* (Mass. 1947), who argues soundly that in the Seventeenth Century:

> The early prince was most decidedly a malcontent avenger, who still kept the markings of his Kydian ancestry . . . This period did not see the prince in isolation as a figure to psychologise or dissect . . . it saw him as a mortal upon whom the ghost of his murdered father had laid a terrible command.
>
> (pp. 9–10)

8. See B.L. Joseph, *Conscience and the King.*
9. D.G. Allen, 'The Aesthetic paradox in *Hamlet*', *Journal of Aesthetics and Art Criticism.*
10. Theodore Roethke, *Collected Poems*, (London, 1968), p. 45

11. So it is unlike the duck-rabbit example, and, in this respect, unlike 'Valediction: forbidding mourning'. But it just happens to be the case that, with the Donne example certainly, the differing interpretations are (necessarily) mutually exclusive and destructive. The differing perceived moods of 'My Papa's Waltz' can intermingle.

12. Though we may think of George Herbert's 'Easter' as a love poem before we know its title or its author, it is very difficult to do so once we are given that information.

13. The discovery of Kurt Vonnegut's political convictions and his experiences during the Second World War, particularly in the bombing of Dresden, might be sufficient to reveal to some readers the bitterness and profundity in his novels; but others, impressed by the levity of tone in his comic novels, would consider the information irrelevant.

14. However much Ken Russell might protest that his film *The Devils* is an attack on and an exposure of corruption, the way in which it wallows in its own evil seems too strong a sign of self-indulgence to ignore.

15. We are thinking here of the connotation Davison points out. 'Ball' does have a specific sexual sense which this context inevitably calls to mind, but in giving an account of these lines we would discount it either as irrelevant, or as, finally, incoherent. Nonetheless, it may have a reinforcing effect on our response here.

16. His lack of awareness of the sensuality which pervades the poem is also revealed by his initial description of the lines as 'relatively abstract' and lacking 'sensual appeal'.

17. These implications are of a sort that philosophers would call 'informal' 'pragmatic', or 'contextual'.

18. 'What does "The Windhover" mean?' in *Immortal Diamond*, ed. N. Weyand (London, 1949), p. 295

19. 'Aesthetic — Theological thoughts on "The Windhover" ', trans. G.H. Hartman and C. Levenson, in *Hopkins*, ed. G.H. Hartman (New Jersey, 1966) p. 78

20. For example, those who suggest that the bird's fulfilling its natural function is both a praise and an echo of Christ, see E. Ruggles, *Gerard Manley Hopkins* (New York, 1944). It is sometimes suggested that the bird's warrior-like existence symbolises Christ's war on evil. But are mice and small birds then symbols of evil?

21. Though, of course, some fail, and some, e.g. John Ashbery, and in a different way, Charles Olson, don't make the attempt.

22. This is the case with his 'dark sonnets': 'They obviously fall into what is well known as the season of dry and dark faith, a season during which most good people are deprived of all the old sensible delights they formerly enjoyed when thinking of God and all his saints. Faith is left without its natural supports *and never wavers* — and so prepares the way for a fuller dependence on God. (Our italics) M.C. D'Arcy, foreword to J. Pick, *Gerard Manley Hopkins*.

23. Empson himself is a past master at interpreting both sorts of incoherence, cf. in particular his sixth type of ambiguity.

24. There is, for example, a critic who believes that the disparities between Natasha's various ages reveal Tolstoy's sense of 'open' time. Y. Birman, *Russkaya Literature*, III, 1966, referred to by R.F. Christian, *Tolstoy: A Critical Introduction* (Cambridge, 1969), p. 138

25. *The Function of Criticism* (Denver, 1957), pp. 127–35. His argument seems to suggest that the poem is incoherent, but he does not consider accounts such as Empson's. Winters is rare amongst critics in that he explicitly recognises that the windhover is a bird of prey, and that this is a problem in interpreting the poem.

26. Suggested by a note, D. McChesney, *A Hopkins Commentary* (London, 1968) p. 68

27. Huxley does not present his arguments but we can hypothesise about the account such a reader might give of his discomfort.

28. C.S. Lewis, *Preface to Paradise Lost* (Oxford, 1942), p. 134

29. Of course, Leavis, in his wholehearted enthusiasm for Lawrence, endorses his values; it is possible that we accept Leavis just as we accept Lawrence, because of our moral predisposition.

Chapter 2: *The nature of critical arguments*

1. F.R. Leavis, *Revaluation* (London 1936) and R.H. Fogle, *The Imagery of Keats and Shelley* (Hamden, Conn. 1963)

2. Leavis, *Revaluation*, p. 171

3. Fogle, *The Imagery of Keats and Shelley* pp. 265–6

4. Leavis, *Revaluation*, p. 172

5. Cf. ' "Thought" and Emotional Quality', *Scrutiny*, 1945. Reprinted in *Selections from Scrutiny*

6. Yet there are few real similarities between, say, lovers and compasses, which Donne links in a powerful image where the leaning together of the compass arms represents physically and so gives substance and reality to the way in which the lovers' thoughts and feelings are inclined towards each other.

7. Suppose we had an inelastic rope, approximately 25,000 miles in length, fitting tightly round the circumference of a smooth, hard sphere, roughly the size of the earth. Now suppose we increased the length of the rope by a yard. If the rope retained its circular shape, what would be the average distance between it and the surface of the globe? Surely an imperceptibly small distance? No, about six inches.

   Cf. N. Malcolm, *Ludwig Wittgenstein: A Memoir* (London, 1958), p. 53

8. In conversation: only those who have heard Frank Cioffi talk about

criticism will appreciate our debt to him.

9. A. Isenberg, 'Critical Communication', *Philosophical Review*, 1949.
10. We do not need to hypothesise such an appeal in relation to the poem. See W.K. Wimsatt, *The Verbal Icon* (New York, 1954), pp. 115–16:

> In Shelley's 'Ode to the West Wind' the shifts in imagery of the second stanza, the pell-mell raggedness and confusion of loose clouds, decaying leaves, angels and Maenads with hair uplifted, the dirge, the dome, the vapors, and the enjambment from tercet to tercet combine to give an impression beyond statement of the very wildness, the breath and power which is the vehicle of the poem's radical metaphor.

> Fogle himself also gestures towards this position.

11. Kant himself appreciated this problem:

> By a principle of taste I mean a principle under the condition of which we could subsume the concept of an object and thus infer, by means of syllogism, that the object is beautiful. But that is absolutely impossible. For I must immediately feel pleasure in the representation of the object, and of that I can be persuaded by no grounds of proof whatever. Although as Hume says, all critics can reason more plausibly than cooks, yet the same fate awaits them. They cannot expect the determining ground of their judgement (to be derived) from the force of the proofs, but only from the reflection of the subject upon its own proper state (of pleasure or pain), all precepts and rules being rejected . . . But although critics can and ought to pursue their reasonings so that our judgement of taste may be corrected and extended, it is not with a view to set forth the determining ground of this kind of aesthetical judgements in a universally applicable formula, which is impossible.

> *Critique of Judgement*, trans. J.H. Bernard (1892; reprint ed. New York, 1951), pp. 127–8

12. See Leavis, 'Literary Criticism and Philosophy'.
13. *Ibid*.

> But these are not only possible but useful in non-academic criticism. Librarians are often asked to select books for persons they know and for persons in various categories. Cinema managers do a similar thing in booking films. A T.V. play reader might feel justified in returning unread a modern verse drama, and would very probably be right. The possibility of arguing in this way is also the greater the more traditional the culture in which the accepting critic works.

14. R. Wellek, 'Literary Criticism and Philosophy', *Scrutiny*, 1937.
15. Leavis, 'Literary Criticism and Philosophy'.
16. '[The Critic] must be on his guard against abstracting improperly from what is in front of him and against any premature or irrelevant

generalizing — of it or from it. His first concern is to enter into posses-
sion of the given poem.'

Leavis, 'Reality and Sincerity', *Scrutiny*, 1952

17. Cf. Leavis, 'Reality and Sincerity'.
18. See Colin Radford 'Characterising-Judgements and their Causal Coun-
    terparts', *Analysis,* January 1971, pp. 65–75
19. L. Wittgenstein, *Lectures and Conversations on Aesthetics, Psychology
    and Religious Belief*, ed. C. Barrett (Oxford, 1967), p. 4
20. Wordsworth seems to have been aware of this when he spoke of the
    'foolish hope of *reasoning* him[the reader] into an approbation' of his
    Lyrical Ballads. Preface to the *Lyrical Ballads* (1800).
21. 'Literary Criticism and Philosophy'.
22. When making an adverse judgement on Tennyson he says:

    'The particularity of "the happy Autumn-fields", "the first beam
    glittering on a sail", and the casement that "slowly fades a glimmer-
    ing square", and so on, is only speciously of the kind in question.'
    ' "Thought" and Emotional Quality', *Scrutiny*, 1945.

23. *Ibid.*
24. Consider 'concreteness', for example:

    'Whenever in poetry we come on places of especially striking 'con-
    creteness' — places where the verse has such life and body that we
    hardly seem to be reading arrangements of words . . .'.

    'Imagery and Movement', *Scrutiny*, 1945

    'The distinctively tactual 'plump' clearly owes its full-bodied con-
    creteness to the pervasive strength in the use of words . . .',

    'Mr. Eliot and Milton' in *The Common Pursuit*, (London, 1952), p.
    16

25. But hasn't Leavis on occasions changed his mind? He has; but his
    criterion of what is correct is what he sees now, rather as the criterion
    for the correctness of a man's account of his dream is, according to
    Wittgenstein, what a man says. *Philosophical Investigations* (Oxford,
    1958) Part II, vii, xi, p. 222
26. 'Literary Criticism and Philosophy'.
27. Anyone who still feels — as some critics may — that the main question in
    the Leavis–Fogle argument — *viz.* 'who is right?' — has not been
    answered, is ignoring the implications of the philosophical account we
    have given for the critical one. In this and similar disputes there can be
    no substitute for returning to the poem and trying to get clear how we
    feel about it; and although the certainty of our feelings may lead us to
    express them, properly, in an objective idiom, there can be no vindica-
    tion of that idiom beyond the other readers' responding similarly.
28. *Poems and Critics*; ed. Christopher Ricks, (London, 1966), p. 30
29. Critics will appeal to the harsh or unpleasant sound of 'gullible' to

explain its unsuitability for Milton's purposes. They may well be right. But may it not be the case that 'gullible' sounds unpleasant because its connotations are unpleasant, and much less pleasant than those of 'credulous'? We are reminded of the apocryphal story concerning the Spanish lady learning English who complained that it was an ugly language. She reluctantly agreed that there were some beautiful words and phrases in the language and mentioned one that she had come across but not understood. It was 'cellar door.' Why then does 'gullible' sound unpleasant? Perhaps this question, like the question 'Why is "frock" being replaced by "dress"?', takes us beyond the realm of literary and critical enquiry.

30. Cf. *The Idler*, 60, (*Ibid.*) Vol. II, p. 189
31. *Life of Pope*, in *Lives of the English Poets*, ed. G.B. Hill (1905), Vol. III, pp. 230–2
32. It is not like feeling sick, 'feeling' that it is all that drink that is making one feel sick, and deciding that it is indeed all that drink that is making one feel sick because one has noticed that a lot of drink has had this effect on one in the past.

Chapter 3: The logical richness of criticism; an analysis of Ricks on Tennyson

1. P.H. Nowell-Smith has noticed exactly the same problem arising in analytic philosophy of history. (In an unpublished paper.) He further suggests that the practical need to concentrate on short and so crucial, problematic passages may help to explain a thirty-year old, continuing preoccupation with a single question, *viz.* do historians' explanations conform to the 'covering law' model?
2. As for example Morris Weitz claims in *Hamlet and the Philosophy of Literary Criticism* (1965).
3. Which is denied by, e.g. A. Isenberg, 'Critical Communication', *Philosophical Review* (July 1949) (see below); John Casey, *The Language of Criticism* (Oxford 1966) (see below); and, on occasions, L. Wittgenstein, cf. *Lectures and Conversations on Aesthetics*, II §§ 14–20, esp §§ 19, §§ 36–39, III, §§ 9–11.

   Frank Cioffi, many times in discussion — who has now recanted on this, see 'Aesthetic Experience and Aesthetic Perplexity', *Acta Philosophica Sennica*, Vol. 28, nos. 1–3.
4. Christopher Ricks, *Poems and Critics*, (London, 1966), pp. 23–8
5. See Chapter one, p. 20 above.
6. Or someone who disagreed with a critic but hadn't appreciated the points we're making now might in consequence of the compression of the claims reject all that was being said, because he disagreed with one part of it.

7. In making this claim about the ebbing and flowing of feeling in the poem and its connection with the abba rhyme scheme, Ricks is clearly influenced, whether consciously or unconsciously, by his reading of *In Memoriam* as a whole. Certainly his claim would be more plausible if it were one about the rhyme scheme and the ebb and flow of feeling throughout the long poem. We feel that Ricks harms his own cause here by, curiously, choosing as an example of a short poem what is in fact part of a much longer poem: and whilst it is true that the various parts of *In Memoriam* can be seen as individual poems, and were perhaps originally written as such, nonetheless Tennyson attempts to impose a coherent pattern on the whole, and in fact certain phrases of this example are echoed and used again later in the long poem. But Ricks presents this claim to us as one about the individual poem, and it must be examined as such.

8. There are certain typographical conventions in contemporary poetry: a double space between words might express a break in the thought, upper case letters might express greater intensity.

9. So that it would be 'correct' even though it strives to explain what is not the case; that is to say, this section of *In Memoriam* might not succeed in expressing or conveying the ebbing or flowing of Tennyson's grief and hope, but fail to do so despite the tendency of the abba rhyme scheme to do just that (i.e. other factors might overwhelm it).

10. But suppose we try an experiment; we say to people who share Ricks' interpretation: 'Look at the rhyme scheme — can't you see that it contributes to the ebbing and flowing of feeling?' And they might say 'Yes'; but they might be wrong.

11. But again, can't we test the claim that it does help to produce such a feeling, by experiment? We draw attention to the rhyme scheme to someone who is doubtful of the interpretative claim. As a result the interpretative claim strikes him as more plausible. Doesn't this experiment prove that the rhyme scheme does contribute to producing, reinforcing, or making us more aware of the ebb and flow of feeling in the poetry? So isn't the explanatory claim testable, contrary to our previous argument?

   The difficulty here is, how could he have not been aware of the rhyme scheme, or at least if it makes a contribution, how could it have failed to do so for him before the critic pointed out that that's what it does? The reply would be that the critic is educating the reader, he is sensitizing him to the presence of the rhyme scheme so that it has an effect that it did not have on him prior to his reading the critic. (It is difficult to see how he can sensitize the reader to *how* it has its effect, if this is unclear, and it is unclear that it does have an effect.) But now we won't know and won't be able to tell whether the critic has indeed done that, or has over-sensitized and indeed corrupted the reader, that is has created the contribution of the rhyme scheme by suggesting that it has this effect — which suggestion's being accepted by the reader, it does have that effect. In this case the rhyme scheme then does contribute to the ebb and flow of feeling, but its doing this is not as it were an inherent tendency of the rhyme scheme but is something created by the critic.

But how about the critic himself? Didn't the rhyme scheme have an inherent tendency in his case to contribute to the ebb and flow of feeling in the poetry? The answer once again is that since the explanation is untestable, and lacks such inherent plausibility, he too may be the victim of his own ingenuity.

12. Of course we can imagine that Ricks is right about the interpretation of the poem, right that a sensitive man ought to respond as he says he should to the rhyme scheme, and yet be wrong in thinking in the case of some particular sensitive man (e.g. Ricks himself) that the rhyme scheme is doing that work here. It might not do the work for him for some reason (perhaps interference of other factors), indeed it might not do the work for any sensitive man, perhaps because something else is doing the work, and the work of the rhyme scheme is nugatory. But he is committed to the claim that, *caeteris paribus*, the contribution that the rhyme scheme should make in this and perhaps other poems is to reinforce or produce an ebb and flow of feeling, and it will make that contribution for the sensitive man.

13. A. Isenberg, 'Critical Communication.'

14. This man is certainly odd, but no odder than Hegel, who was amused by the way a line makes a tangent to a circle.

15. A similar effect was gained by an American Marines' Band in an Edinburgh military tattoo, who played a blues number — 'I love to see the evening sun go down'. They began in strict march time with the percussion section, and when the tune came in the delight of the audience was immediate and its source transparent — the incongruity between what they were playing on the one hand, and who was playing it and how it was being played on the other.

16. *Poetics*, trans. T.S. Dorsch (Penguin 1965), p. 67

17. Which shows how in appreciating works of art we treat them as historical objects.

18. This is not an imaginary example. R.H. Fogle comments in precisely this way on Keats in *The Imagery of Keats and Shelley*, p. 63

19. We could ask Ricks here, as he asks Robert Lowell, how much he or even Tennyson can 'legitimately expect us to know'. *New Statesman*, 26th March, 1965.

20. We have shown that the effect, the contribution of this aspect of the poem is problematic and ultimately not decidable. How self-indulgent and uncritical it is, then, to commit oneself — not merely in connection with a particular work but as a general thesis — to the view that what is important in art, and in literature in particular, is its 'form' or 'structure', whatever these protean terms may mean (so long as they exclude content). These large-scale critical theories, if *critical* theories they are, are self-indulgent, and the more particular claims and theories which they produce are characteristically implausible, but untestable. One can only speculate as to why they should attract; perhaps there is an

essentialist argument at work here, that since it cannot be the content of works of literature which distinguish them from writing which is not art, it must be something else.

21. But couldn't a man deny, resist, suppress the fact that he was affected by the rhyme scheme, or by rhyme schemes in general? It is not just because a man is less likely to have repressed feelings about rhyme schemes than he is to have repressed feelings about death that we do not mention it in the text. It is rather that he cannot have the immediate awareness of the effect that this rhyme scheme has on him which he can have concerning his feeling about death. And it is this notion of direct awareness which we are pursuing here.

22. The thesis that the rhyme scheme gets its effect in the way the nitrous oxide gets its effect is not a general one about rhyme schemes, but only about this rhyme scheme in this example. One can imagine a rhyme scheme getting its effect by parodying another rhyme scheme, achieving a kind of amusement where one wouldn't be affected by the rhyme scheme as one is here, but by recognizing — perceiving — that it is parodying another rhyme scheme.

23. Cf. Casey, *The Language of Criticism*, pp. 8, 71, 90, 95

24. This sometimes fine distinction, which can be so important, is explicitly recognised, and discussed, by Herman Melville in the chapter 'The Whiteness of the Whale' in *Moby Dick*. Appreciating how difficult it may be to draw on occasions, he writes in a footnote thus:

> With reference to the Polar bear, it may possibly be urged by him who would fain go still deeper into this matter, that it is not the whiteness, separately regarded, which heightens the intolerable hideousness of that brute; for, analysed, that heightened hideousness, it might be said, only arises from the circumstance, that the irresponsible ferociousness of the creature stands invested in the fleece of celestial innocence and love; and hence, by bringing together two such opposite emotions in our minds, the Polar bear frightens us with so unnatural a contrast. But even assuming all this to be true; yet, were it not for the whiteness, you would not have that intensified terror.

> *Moby Dick* ed. R. Lee, (London, 1975), pp. 164–5

25. Unless, of course, he is repressing something. But even if we suppress our awareness of the subterranean idea or of our response to it and our awareness of that response, we are suppressing or repressing a direct immediate awareness of these things, i.e. the idea, our awareness of how it affects us, and its 'affecting' us.

Chapter 4: Are there any necessary conditions of excellence in art?

1.   'Yet when I speak thus slightly of dramatic rules, I cannot but recollect how much wit and learning may be produced against me; before such authorities I am afraid to stand, not that I think the present question one to be decided by mere authority, but because it is to be suspected that these precepts have not been so easily received but for better reasons than I have been able to find.'

   Ibid. p. 80

2. As it may have been for, e.g., the French classical dramatists.
3. What Kenneth Burke calls 'categorical expectations', *Counter-statement* (California, 1931), pp. 38–9
4.   'It ought to be the first endeavour of a writer to distinguish nature from custom, or that which is established because it is right, from that which is right, because it is established; that he may neither violate essential principles by a desire of novelty, nor debar himself from the attainment of beauties within his view by a needless fear of breaking rules which no literary dictator had authority to enact'.

   Rambler, No. 156, (*Ibid.*) Vol. V, p. 70

5. It might be thought to be a sufficient condition of a modern comedy's being good as well but if it is, it is at least necessary. A comedy cannot be a good comedy if it is not funny.
6. Comedies were in fact traditionally believed to be lesser plays, a tradition which perhaps stems from Aristotle.
7. Although of course we must remember that it is theoretically possible that at a higher level of abstraction these conditions might transform themselves into necessary conditions.
8. It might be objected here that there are many works which lack technical skills which we do not describe as unskilful. The early primitives, such as Duccio, could not depict perspective with any accuracy or sophistication, but this was only because the idea of perspective was not yet developed, nor were the necessary techniques. As for artists to whom those techniques were available but who did not make use of them, e.g. 'action' painters, we cannot infer, as we can with the modern primitives, from the lack of skills in their painting to a lack of skill. Theirs is a self-conscious decision to produce non-representational works which do not require such techniques, though they make other artistic demands on their creators.
9. There are some artists who have exploited the style of the primitive painters; L.S. Lowry is perhaps an example. Their work may be visually indistinguishable from that of the primitives, but it inevitably loses the primitive's innocence precisely by its deliberate attempt to capture it. There are of course people who enjoy the *faux-naïveté* of these skilful painters.

10. Unless a painting is classified as primitive only because the life-style of the painter and the main body of his work are characteristic of a primitive, e.g. Henri Rousseau's 'Tropical Storm with Tiger'.
11. 'The Art of Fiction', from *Henry James: Selected Fiction*, ed. Edel (London, 1953), p. 599
12. Monroe Beardsley, *Aesthetics: Problems in the philosophy of criticism* (New York, 1958), pp. 457–460
13. Frank Cioffi, 'Intention and Interpretation in Criticism', *Proceedings of the Aristotelian Society, 1963–4*

> A further problem is created for Beardsley by our distinguishing between originals and forgeries. Our feeling that there is a great difference isn't to be explained by the minute physical differences but by their genesis. Beardsley's anti-intentionalism commits him to the view that if there are no 'observable' differences between two such works, then there is no aesthetic difference between them. Suppose, he says, there is 'no difference in their internal characteristics, so that no one could tell them apart just by looking at them. Then, I suggest, this amounts to saying that there is no *aesthetic* reason for the judgement (that one is better than the other) . . . two objects that do not differ in any observable qualities cannot differ in aesthetic value'.
>
> *Aesthetics: Problems in the philosophy of criticism* p. 503

14. Clive Bell, *Art*, (Reprint, New York, 1958), blurb.
15. He slides from one phrase to the other in a single sentence, *ibid*, p. 17
16. *Philosophical Investigations*, I, §67
17. *Australasian Journal of Philosophy*, 1960.
18. 'If ["people who respond immediately and surely to works of art"] are not curious about the nature of their emotion, nor about the quality common to all objects that provoke it, they have my sympathy, and, as what they say is often charming and suggestive, my admiration too. Only let no-one suppose that what they write and talk is aesthetics; it is criticism, or just "shop".

> *Art*, p. 16

19. What then of fakes? Bell says with Beardsley that if a fake 'were an absolutely exact copy, clearly it would be as moving as the original'. However, he recognises that fakes seldom, if ever, are as moving as originals, i.e. we don't respond to or value them as we do originals, and concludes, 'Evidently, it is impossible to imitate a work of art exactly; and the differences between the copy and the original, minute though they may be, exist and are felt immediately' (p. 49). Bell explains these postulated differences and their postulated consequences for our feelings about a work in terms of 'some curious mental and emotional power' (p. 50) which the original artist has and his imitator usually does not have. Undoubtedly and in most cases these minute physical differences do exist and they may have immediate consequences for our appreciation of the works. But they need not always exist and even where they do, the true explanation of our feeling about a fake is perhaps rather to be found in its being a *fake*, i.e. in its genesis and

particularly in the motives, and inspiration and originality of the artist as compared with his imitators. Now that there is such a difference— or rather, as Bell sees it, that there is an 'emotional' difference between the original artist and his imitator, he sees as a metaphysical hypothesis. But the metaphysical hypothesis is in fact that there are always physical differences between originals and fakes and these have an immediate effect. This hypothesis is a corollary of the doctrine of significant form. Cf. Colin Radford, 'Fakes', *Mind*, 1978.

20. Monroe Beardsley, 'The Discrimination of Aesthetic Enjoyment', *British Journal of Aesthetics*, 1963.
21. This indeed may explain part of the appeal of significant form. Bell's Bloomsbury audience was probably reacting against the Victorian interest in painting which was vulgarly narrative.
22. A similar account, but one which only mentions unity, is provided in 'The Discrimination of Aesthetic Enjoyment'.
23. Bell, who was very aware of the aesthetic difference between art and nature strove to find it in the artist's 'emotion'. Natural objects may be beautiful, but only works which are the expression of the artist's emotion can have 'significant form' *Art*, p. 43
24. The diversity of art forms, the existence of so many aesthetic objects which are not works of art, the differences in and changes of aesthetic taste, should all warn us that a general account of what is aesthetic and what is not would involve a great deal of painstaking study. Wittgenstein's dictum 'Don't think but look' (*Lectures and Conversations on Aesthetics*., p. 66) is particularly relevant here. And it would also raise, after the descriptive work had been done, very difficult normative questions concerning which of those experiences and reasons some of us call aesthetic should nevertheless be excluded. For discussion of a similar problem, but in a quite different field, *viz.*, knowledge, see 'Knowledge — by examples', Colin Radford, *Analysis*, 1966.
25. 'On the Generality of Critical Reasons', *Journal of Philosophy*, 1962, p. 4
26. 'The Discrimination of Aesthetic Enjoyment', p. 297
27. Henry Watson Fowler, *Modern English Usage*, (Oxford, 1940), pp. 319–20
28. Beardsley himself proposes this solution *en passant* in 'The Classification of Critical Reasons', *Journal of Aesthetic Education*, 1968.
29. 'The Discrimination of Aesthetic Enjoyment', p. 297
30. Beardsley might deny that this was his position, but it is one to which he is committed by his thesis about fakes.
31. Cf. Wittgenstein on 'Seeing an aspect', *Lectures and Conversations on Aesthetics* II §xi.
32. Isn't it unlikely that two persons seriously interested in this music would engage in such a dispute? Yet Beardsley's metacritical position would make this difficult to explain. All he could say is that critics intuitively recognise that this is a hard case. But another explanation is that they feel that works of art which attain a certain stature cannot even in

principle be ranked; their merits, virtues, qualities, etc. — even when what we are putting side by side are the complexities of the two works — are incommensurable.

33. He is worried, though, by the fact that long novels are 'always in danger of dissipating attention by spreading it out into our usual diffuse awareness of the environment' (p. 528). But surely this is the kind of example that should lead him to revise his account of what aesthetic experiences are like?

34. In fact, Beardsley may not be committing himself to either of the causal theses, nor to either of the constitutive ones. He is almost certainly unclear about what claims he is making.

35. Consider the perhaps quasi-aesthetic response to certain tastes, e.g., 'this is bitter'. Don't we have here a response which indissolubly weds our apprehension of some feature of something eaten and our dislike of it. But some people like, say, bitter chocolate, and it taste *bitter* to them. But someone might now say, ' "Bitter" foods which are liked by certain persons taste different to those who like them from how they taste to those who dislike them'. (So that 'bitter' has a different meaning in these cases.) But it should be clear that this thesis, if not vacuous, is virtually untestable. The only sort of evidence that would bear on the truth of the hypothesis, would be the testimony of those who liked some bitter foods and not others, or, perhaps better, who liked bitter foods in certain contexts and combinations and not in others. But of course anyone committed to the metaphysical thesis could discount the testimony if it seemed to tell against his thesis. And in this way the metaphysical thesis tends to vacuity.

Chapter 5: Reasons, causes and targets

1. For example, A. Isenberg, see below.
2. 'On the Generality of Critical Reasons', *Journal of Philosophy*, 1962.
3. It will be remembered that Beardsley denies this, at least he says that there are no grounds for having an aesthetic preference for originals rather than indistinguishable forgeries. However, he could be wrong about this and right about the causal principle, for there could be — and we have argued that there are — aesthetic differences between original and forgeries, however perfect, and there must always be differences in their genesis which in principle are detectable by scientific and historical investigation.
4. 'On the Generality of Critical Reasons'.
5. See Isenberg, below.
6. See p. 79 above.
7. A point insisted on in his own by Leavis in his reply to Wellek.
8. Beardsley 'The Discrimination of Aesthetic Enjoyment', *British Journal of Aesthetics*, 1963. p. 479

9. See our discussion of Ricks' claim about the 'subterranean idea' in his Tennyson passage, pp. 105–14 above.
10. Cf. Colin Radford, 'Characterising-Judgements and their Causal Counterparts', *Analysis*, January 1971, pp. 65–75
11. See our discussion of Stallworthy, pp. 69–83 above.
12. A. Isenberg, 'Critical Communication', *Philosophical Review* (July, 1949), References to the reprint in *Philosophy Looks at the Arts* (New York 1962, *ed.* Joseph Margolis. This article makes points reminiscent of the work of Wittgenstein, though this was not published in 1949.
13. Peter Cheeseman, Victoria Theatre, Stoke-on-Trent. In conversation.
14. Corporation Galleries.
15. As, indeed, is Frank Cioffi. In many conversations.

Index

A Hopkins Commentary 165n
A Shaping Joy 63
Achievement of D.H. Lawrence, The 39
Aesthetics 132 f
Allen, D.G. 25, 26, 163n
ambiguity 27, 29, 30, 35, 38, 61, 106, 125
An Approach to Hamlet 162n
Animal Farm 18-22, 91
Anna Karenina 137
'Ariel' 23
Arnold, Matthew 4
Aristotle 8, 9, 13, 14, 102, 112, 120, 163n, 172n
Art of Fiction, The ed. Edel 173n
Art 129, 173n, 174n
Ashbery, John 164n
aspect, seeing an 28, 30, 32, 174n
Austen, Jane 127, 155
Austin, J.L. 46
Ayer, A.J. 51

Beardsley, Monroe 127, 131-8, 140-6, 148, 149, 156, 173n, 174n, 175n
   Aesthetics 173n
  'The Classification of Critical Reasons' 174n
  'The Discrimination of Aesthetic Enjoyment' 174n, 176n
  'On the Generality of Critical Reasons' 174n, 175n
Beethoven, L. 136, 162n
Bell, Clive 129-31
Bernard, J.H. 166n
Birman, Y. 165n
Bowers, F. 163n
Brecht, B. 120
Brooks, Cleanth 63-4
Browning, Robert 33

Burke, K. 172n

Casey, John 168n, 171n
causal 12, 45, 62, 78, 82, 85, 93-5, 101, 108, 110, 111, 138, 145f, 150f
'Characterising-Judgements and their Causal Counterparts' 162n, 167n, 176n
Cheeseman, Peter 176n
Christian, R.F. 165n
Cioffi, F. 47, 165n, 168n, 173n, 176n
'The Classification of Critical Reasons' 174n
'Clusters' 129
Common Pursuit, The 57, 167n
Conklin, L.P.S. 163n
Conscience and the King 161n
convention 17, 25, 96
correctness 4, 44, 64, 69, 71f, 115, 145, 148, 154
Counter-statement 172n
credibility 116-20
criteria 54, 77, 115, 122-30, 132f, 144
critical disagreement 6, 8, 27, 38-42, 45f, 98, 115, 122f, 151, 156-7
critical judgements, causal dimension of 12, 45, 62, 78f, 101f, 145f
  moral dimension of 3f, 39-43, 111f, 133, 142
  singular 77, 82-3, 115, 141, 148, 155
critical terms 50, 51, 53, 122, 123, 127, 128, 157
Critique of Judgement 166n
Croce 152

D'Arcy, M.C. 164n
Davison, D. 31, 32, 164n
Day Lewis, C. 32, 33
description 6, 8, 10, 84f, 92-3, 129, 149, 152-3
Dickens, Charles 161n
'The Discrimination of Aesthetic Enjoyment' 174n, 176n
Donne, John 28, 63, 156-7, 164n, 165n

El Greco 153
Eliot, T.S. 58, 85
emotion 96, 147
Empson, W. 34, 35, 37, 38, 165n
'Entertaining Mr. Sloane' 123
evaluation 6, 10, 11, 39f, 62, 85, 89f, 115, 123, 127, 132, 139, 144f
explanation 4-6, 10f, 16, 22, 56, 62f
Eyck, Van, Hubert 24

'Fakes' 174n
Fogle, R.H. 44-50, 53-6, 115
Fowler, H.W. 135, 174n
Function of Criticism, The 165n

Gainsborough, T. 2
  'Sarah Siddons' 2
Gasking, D. 129
  Clusters' 129
Gerard Manley Hopkins, Priest and Poet 35
Giorgione 154
Gray, T. 102
Guardini, R. 35
Gulliver's Travels 21, 22

Hallam, Arthur 85-91, 105-7, 113
Hamlet 8f., 24-6, 86-7, 124, 161n, 162n, 163n
Hamlet and the Philosophy of Literary Criticism 168n
Hare, R.M. 51
Hartman, G. 164n
Herbert, George 164n
historicity of art objects 24, 135

Hitler 42
Homer 103
Hooker 57
Hopkins, G.M. 34-6, 105
Housman, 63
Hume, D. 51
Huxley, A. 39

'Imagery and Movement' 167n
Imagery of Keats and Shelley, The 165n, 170n
imagination 2, 4
Immortal Diamond 164n
In Memoriam 85, 88, 91, 93-5, 106, 109
intention 4, 12, 20-2, 113, 127-8
interpretation 1f, 18f, 69, 77, 83, 84, 89-93, 96f
'Intention and Interpretation in Criticism' 173n
Isenberg, A. 47, 148-53, 155-7, 166n, 168n, 170n, 175n, 176n

James, Henry 105, 126-7
Johnson, S. 78-9, 115f, 145, 155
Joseph, B.L. 161n, 163n

Kant, E. 166n
Keats, John 57, 103, 170n
Knights, L.C. 161n, 162n
'Knowledge-by Examples' 174n

Landseer, E. 128
Language of Criticism, The 168n, 171n
Lawrence, D.H. 23, 39-43, 155, 165n
Leavis, F.R. 5, 39-57, 62, 115, 157, 162n, 163n, 165nf
'Lectures and Conversations in Aesthetics' 167n, 174n
Levenson, C. 164n
Lewis, C.S. 40, 57, 61, 165n
Lovelace 30
Lowell, Robert 170n
Lowry, L.S. 172n
Lyrical Ballads 167n

Ludwig Wittgenstein: A Memoir 165n

McChesney, D. 165n
de Madariaga, S. 162n
MacIntyre, A. 163n
Margolis, J. 176n
Marvell, Andrew, 31, 33
Melville, H. 171n
metaphor 32, 33, 43, 54, 63, 89, 90
Michelangelo 162n
Milton 40, 56f, 66-7, 150
monolithic 7, 85, 141
Moore, G.E. 51
moral 3f, 39-43, 111f, 133, 142
Mozart 136
Murry, J.M. 161n

necessary conditions 115, 120f, 141-2
New Critic 106
norm 149, 150, 151
normative 62, 80, 99, 101, 105, 145-6, 157
Nowell-Smith, Patrick 168n

Olson, Charles, 164n
'On the Generality of Critical Reasons' 174n, 175n
originality 127, 128, 133
Orton, Joe 123
Orwell, George 20

Paradise Lost 40, 56, 57, 61, 65, 67
Pick, J. 35, 36, 37, 38, 165n
Philosophical Investigations 167n, 173n
Plath, Sylvia 23
Pleydell-Pearce 141
Poetic Image, The 32
Poetics 8, 9, 117
Poetry of Andrew Marvell, The 31
Pope, Alexander 102, 146, 147, 153
portraits 2, 3, 4
practical critics 6, 85, 121

Preface to Paradise Lost 57
Preface to Shakespeare 117
proof. 4, 11, 14, 15, 22, 49, 55f, 112, 151, 157

Radford, C.J. 162n, 167n, 174n, 176n
'Reality and Sincerity' 54, 169n
Rembrandt 3, 128, 130, 153
response 2, 3, 5, 12, 13, 14, 26, 27, 40f, 67f, 82f, 139f, 147-50, 154-7
Revaluation 165n
rhythm 4
Ricks, C. 56f, 84f, 91f, 145, 167nf
Roethke, T. 27, 30, 163n
Rousseau, H. 173n
Ruggles, H. 164n
Russell, Ken 164n

Schoder, R.V. 35
scholarship 1, 5, 25, 26
seeing an aspect 28, 30, 32
sensibility 3, 5
sentimentality 3
Seven Types of Ambiguity 34
Shakespeare, W. 17, 24, 115, 116
Shelley, P.B. 44-56, 166n
'significant form' 129-31
singular 77-83, 115, 141, 148, 155
Stalin 20
Stallworthy, J. 69-83, 176n
sufficient conditions 124
Swift 21, 22, 23

target 110, 147, 148
Tennyson, A. 84-98, 106, 112, 113, 169n, 176n
' "Thought" and Emotional Quality' 54, 165n
Thomson, J. 87
Tolstoy 37, 137, 165n
tragedy 8-10, 11, 13-15, 24-6, 86-7, 124
truth 4, 5, 11f, 25, 42, 51, 54, 64f, 74-8, 81, 85, 90, 98, 101, 118

understanding 1, 2, 5, 15, 16, 22,
    81
unities 115-23

Van Eyck, Hubert 24
Verbal Icon, The 166n
*Vision and Revision in Yeats' Last
    Poems* 69
Vonnegut, K. 164n

War and Peace 37, 137

Weitz, Morris 168n
Wellek, R. 5, 49, 166n, 176n
Weyand, N. 164n
Wimsatt, W.K. 166n
Winters, Y. 37, 165n
Wittgenstein, L. 52, 110, 129, 140,
    167n, 174n
Wordsworth, W. 86, 167n

Yeats, E.B. 68-82